STREET FURNITURE

LYNN PEARSON

ACKNOWLEDGEMENTS

I should like to thank the following for their support and help with this project: John Bundock, Sue Hudson, Simon Inglis, Ian Macky, Ted McAvoy, Steve Marland, Rachel Martin, Kathryn Morrison, Stephen Veitch, Mark Whyman and Nick Wright.

Every attempt has been made to seek permission for copyright material used in this book. However, if we have inadvertently used copyright material without permission or acknowledgement we apologise and will make the necessary correction at the first opportunity.

First published 2022

Amberley Publishing
The Hill, Stroud,
Gloucestershire, GL5 4EP

www.amberley-books.com

ISBN: 978 1 3981 0772 4 (print)
ISBN: 978 1 3981 0773 1 (ebook)

British Library Cataloguing in Publication Data.
A catalogue record for this book is available from the British Library.

Typeset in 10pt on 13pt Celeste.
Typesetting by SJmagic DESIGN SERVICES, India.
Printed in the UK.

CONTENTS

INTRODUCTION

Our ancestors created paths, probably using earlier tracks made by animals, or following the flow of streams and rivers, or shadowing the coastline. They used landscape features to guide them, and later made signs, perhaps cairns or just heaps of stones, to help travellers in bad weather. The Romans built a network of roads, some tracking the routes of older paths, and introduced wayside stone markers – milestones. As the population grew, the road system became more complex; junctions and boundaries developed. Once turnpike roads appeared, from 1706, milestones became commonplace, along with fingerposts (direction posts or signposts) at junctions. With the car – and goods vehicles – came the need for more and better signage, initially supplied by cycling and motoring organisations but later standardised and installed by local authorities. As roads grew more crowded, street lighting also progressed, aiding pedestrians as well as traffic.

Questions of water supply also contributed to the proliferation of items located in and around (and beneath) our streets. By the seventeenth century piped drinking water was available through street pumps, with drinking fountains and horse troughs being introduced in the later nineteenth century. London's innovative sewers took the insalubrious waste underground, but vent shafts ('stink pipes') were still required to disperse gases. Also underground were many of the public conveniences constructed around the end of the nineteenth century, some highly decorative.

Along with the sewers running beneath our pavements are substantial ducts for gas and electricity pipes and cables, later to be joined by telecommunications paraphernalia. These essentials are invisible to the pedestrian, often walking unknowingly only a few inches above. The apparently mundane manhole covers are a sure sign of what lies below, and tell us much about social and industrial history.

Developments in communications are mirrored by changes in street furniture, through the familiar letter box to now-disappearing telephone kiosks and specialist items like police boxes and cabmen's shelters. Transport improvements have bequeathed to us a variety of shelters for tram and bus passengers, some built in elegant ironwork, as well as other evidence of their infrastructure. Modern bus shelters now include advertisements and even digital connectivity; some are part of a new generation of environmentally friendly street furniture.

Above left: Sir Richard Wallace (1818–90), English art collector and philanthropist, lived mainly in Paris. He designed and financed over 100 drinking fountains, installed in the city from 1872 onward and made by the Val d'Osne foundry, around 120 miles (200 km) east of Paris. Wallace was MP for Lisburn, near Belfast, from 1873 to 1885. He donated five fountains to the town in 1876; this example is one of two surviving. (Lynn Pearson)

Above right: A total of 161 pillar boxes were probably cast during the 1936 reign of Edward VIII, but only 138 remain in service. They are distributed throughout the country, with a cluster in Glasgow and just two in Wales. Two foundries supplied the boxes: McDowall, Steven & Co. (Glasgow) and the Carron Company (Falkirk), like this example. The firms are named on the front and rear of bases respectively. (Lynn Pearson)

Our streets are also home to a variety of significant structures including ornamental fountains, statuary, memorials and public art, which generally lie beyond the remit of this book. The public realm becomes more significant than ever in a post-pandemic world, where space is at a premium. Mobile phones have seen some street furniture lose its relevance, as person to person communication supplanted point to point calls – the search for a charging point has replaced the hunt for a phone box. Historic street furniture forms a significant part of our heritage, but is always vulnerable simply due to its position on the ever-changing streets. Alterations to road layouts can see signs and shelters moved or disappear with little comment – something we should always remember when seeking out specific features illustrated here or elsewhere.

Ireland's Department of Posts and Telegraphs (P&T) introduced new telephone boxes from the 1930s onward; they were made either of concrete or timber. This one stands near the village green in Malin (County Donegal), in the far north of Ireland; the P&T sign is missing from its base. Few P&T boxes remain, as most were removed after 2009. (phbcz/Bigstock.com)

The Festival of Britain-inspired *Piazza Fountain* (1962–67) at the Beetham Plaza in central Liverpool was the work of designer and engineer Richard Huws (1902–80). Overlooking the kinetic water fountain are two yellow viewing platforms, the taller one to the rear also being a ventilation shaft for the plaza's underground car park. (Courtesy of Phil Nash under CC 4.0)

This unusual wooden signpost to local pubs stands in Singleton (West Sussex), next to the A286. It was made around the end of the twentieth century by Roger Champion, who for many years was Master Carpenter at the nearby Weald and Downland Living Museum. (Lynn Pearson)

1

STREETS AND SIGNAGE

Our first paths were trodden by hunter-gatherers in the Neolithic period (5000–2500 BC), often using linear routes (trackways) previously formed by animals. Waymarkers may have been natural phenomena like crags, tall trees and ponds. Settlements eventually became connected by a network of trackways, which could be surfaced with wood in wetland areas; many trackways still survive as today's footpaths or roads.

ROMAN ROADS AND MILESTONES

When the Romans invaded Britain during AD 43, their early forays led them along existing broad earth trackways, with detachments of troops sent in advance to clear the ground for the army, its baggage train and wheeled vehicles. Development of the Roman road system followed, when campaigning was not a priority. The network was planned roughly on the basis of existing routes, but realigned where possible in long, straight lengths; changes in direction were achieved with angled turns rather than curves, as they were simpler to construct. Roads were built either sequentially, from one end to the other, or in sections running outward from various military bases. Typically roads had a central raised spine of coarse rubble, flanked by drainage ditches and surfaced (metalled) with compacted sand and gravel, sturdy enough to take heavy wagons. Their width averaged around 16–33 ft (5–10 m), but occasionally reached 328 ft (100 m).

Roman roads were generally marked with milestones, usually cylindrical stone columns inscribed with a dedication to the emperor in power at the time of road building or repair; distances to destinations were not always included. The Roman mile comprised 1,000 double paces, around 0.9 of a modern mile or *c.* 1.5 km, but somewhat variable in practice. Originally there must have been many thousands of milestones in Britain, but only a tiny percentage survive – a total of 117 – and few of them date from the early years of Roman road construction. Perhaps this was too disjointed a process to include milestones. Alternatively, they may only have been introduced by Hadrian around AD 120, or indeed all the older milestones may have been lost. Most of the 96 or so of our remaining inscribed (and therefore dateable) milestones were put up in the years following AD 235,

The Roman milestone at Kirkby Thore, east of Temple Sowerby (Cumbria), is a rarity as it probably stands in its original position. The red sandstone column, around 4 ft 3 in (1.3 m) high, is on the north side of a former Roman road that crossed the Pennines between Scotch Corner (North Yorkshire) and Brougham, near Penrith (Cumbria). (Courtesy of Northernhenge in public domain)

This Roman milestone at Middleton, Kirkby Lonsdale (Cumbria), originally stood on a major Roman road running north to Carlisle (Cumbria). It was found in 1836 and moved to a nearby hilltop, then in 2016 relocated to the churchyard of the Church of the Holy Ghost. (Courtesy of Rosser1954 under CC 4.0)

nearly two centuries after the invasion began. This was the start of a period of instability, when it became more important to demonstrate loyalty to the current emperor by erecting symbols of political allegiance. Cornwall's few recorded milestones were all erected near the beginning of this period.

Just a handful of Britain's surviving Roman milestones stand in or near their original positions, beside roads; the others are in museums or have been incorporated into later buildings. These five in situ milestones are our earliest examples of street furniture. Four can be found in the north of England: two (one a stub) next to the course of Stanegate, a Roman road, near Vindolanda fort and Hadrian's Wall (Northumberland), while two more remain in Cumbria, near Temple Sowerby and at Middleton, north of Kirkby Lonsdale. The fifth milestone is at Stinsford, east of Dorchester (Dorset).

ROADS AND WAYMARKS AFTER THE ROMANS

By the time the Roman economic system disintegrated around 420, at least 10,000 miles (16,000 km) of roads had been built in Britain. After the Romans left the metalled roads were initially used far less, and were not maintained. During the ninth century towns and villages began to spring up away from the old routes, connected by new paths and roads. By medieval times a relatively dense (although mostly non-metalled) road network was in use, with London and major towns as focal points. Within towns, roads were paved, generally with stone slabs but occasionally cobbles. Where travellers needed assistance in finding the way, local people erected waymarkers, such as the series of Christian wayside stone crosses on Dartmoor.

The Teddington Hands fingerpost (1676) in Gloucestershire, seen on a magic lantern slide of *c.* 1900. Its octagonal sandstone column, around 10 ft (3 m) in height, bears an inscription related to the local Attwood family who erected and maintained the post. (Author's personal collection)

The 1686 guidepost at Wroxton (Oxfordshire) seen in a 1930s photograph from a family album. The post is topped by a sundial and ball finial, and three of its four carved hands are visible. (Author's personal collection)

When coach travel became more fashionable in the sixteenth century, along with the use of heavier wagons, further road improvements became essential, as did the need for more direction signs. Although parishes could afford to maintain local roads, the main highways deteriorated significantly during the seventeenth century. At this point waymarks and guideposts, where they existed, were generally erected by local landowners or other interested parties. This resulted in a wide variety of forms and materials, although pointing fingers often featured, either as carved or relief imagery, or in the shaped arms of fingerposts (signposts). The partly wrought-iron Cross Hands fingerpost (1669) at the A44/B408 crossroads south of Chipping Campden (Gloucestershire) was thought to be England's oldest extant signpost until 1980, when it was replaced by a replica.

Surviving early waymarks include the six-armed Teddington Hands signpost (1676), which still stands near its initial position (now the A46/A435 junction) in Gloucestershire; the stone guidepost (1686) at Wroxton (Oxfordshire) on which four carved hands point the way; and the *c.* 1720 stone slab north of Hutton-le-Hole (North Yorkshire), with its pair of pointing hands. Rather smaller are the two mid-eighteenth-century pre-turnpike direction stones near West Chinnock (Somerset), both with guiding hands.

TURNPIKES AND MILESTONES IN THE EIGHTEENTH AND NINETEENTH CENTURIES

An increasing number of direction signs appeared following legislation in 1697 empowering local magistrates to have waymarkers erected at junctions. The roads themselves slowly improved due to the work of numerous turnpike trusts, bodies set up by Acts of Parliament with powers to collect tolls in order to maintain the highway.

Turnpike trusts originated in the 1660s and reached a peak of popularity during the 1750s and 1760s; most of the main routes were turnpikes by 1780. The provision of mile markers along turnpikes had been encouraged from the 1740s, becoming obligatory in 1766, when the trusts were also required to add distances. Guideposts put up by parishes had only to direct travellers to the next market towns, without specifying mileage. In 1773 the General Turnpike Act made fingerposts, displaying both direction and distance, compulsory at highway junctions.

Early turnpike milestones were usually carved from local stone – granite in Cornwall, slate in Cumbria for instance – and square or cylindrical in form. Angled faces, easier to read at speed, later became popular; similarly, clearer Arabic characters replaced Roman numerals. Towards the end of the eighteenth century, as their original wording started to erode, trusts began to bolt iron plates with incised lettering over the stones. Eventually, for even greater clarity, cast-iron plates with relief lettering were introduced around the turn of the century. Completely cast-iron mileposts appeared in the early nineteenth century.

There is a huge and delightful variety in the designs and inscriptions of milestones and mileposts, ranging from simple metal markers to substantial stone obelisks and columns,

The early nineteenth-century milestone at Shaldon Bridge (Devon) shows distances in miles, furlongs (220 yards) and perches (one-fortieth of a furlong). The statute mile, a standard 1,760 yards, was introduced in 1593. The earliest recorded instance of a road being marked in miles was the Dover to Canterbury road (Kent) in 1633. (Courtesy of Partonez under CC 4.0)

Above left: This cast-iron, Gothic milestone (1836) in the centre of Bridgend (Mid Glamorgan) is one of a series in a similar style located along what was originally the A48, once the main route from south-west England to South Wales. (Courtesy of FruitMonkey under CC 4.0)

Above right: This small, cast-iron milestone (1897) on the Isle of Mull (Argyll and Bute) marks a point between Salen on the east coast and Fionnphort – for the Iona ferry – to the west. Like several of similar twin-oval design on the island, the mainland nearby and in Northumberland, it was made by Smith, Patterson's Pioneer Foundry of Blaydon (Tyne and Wear). (Courtesy of DeFacto under CC 4.0)

the latter types often funded by private donors during the late eighteenth century. Some of the most unusual are the six elaborate mileposts of the Stratford to Long Compton turnpike in Warwickshire, erected around 1818. The ornate cast- and wrought-iron posts, 9 ft (2.7 m) in height, bore wooden destination boards; the ironwork probably came from a foundry in Stratford-upon-Avon.

Thomas Telford (1757–1834), civil engineer and road builder, designed a distinctive new milestone for his London to Holyhead road. Its construction was authorised by Parliament in 1815, making it the first publicly funded road since the Roman era. Telford's milestones used hard-wearing limestone from Anglesey, cut into a tapering shape with a gently pointed head and fitted with a cast-iron plate on the front bearing lettering. Several examples survive, mostly west of Shrewsbury.

Turnpikes declined as railway use increased, and major road maintenance (along with direction signage) became county council responsibilities in 1888; some councils then adopted a uniform design for their mileposts. Many milestones were lost or defaced during the Second World War as they bore place names.

Boot scrapers were important from the late eighteenth century, when urban strolling became fashionable and pedestrians had to deal with the dirt, mess and mud of the streets. Like these cast-iron, saw-edged examples, they were often located in niches beside front doors and could be very ornate. (Lynn Pearson)

ROAD SURFACES IN THE LATE NINETEENTH CENTURY

Even before the arrival of the motor car in the mid- to late 1890s, Britain's roads, particularly in urban areas, were struggling to cope with the increasing amount of horse-drawn traffic. Around 100,000 horses then worked in London, requiring the daily removal of three to four cartloads of horse dung for every mile of major highway. Road surfaces were problematic. The main options were stone setts (cobbles), wood paving (quieter in use by wheeled vehicles, but slippery for horses when wet) and macadam, the invention of Scottish road engineer John Loudon McAdam (1756–1836). It comprised layers of small stones and gravel, compacted by traffic or steamroller. Macadamised surfaces were dusty when dry and muddy (also unhygienic, due to the dung) when wet. Rural roads were often simply unbound stones. Eventually road surfaces were sealed, initially by spraying macadam with tar. A better solution was tarmacadam – tarmac – a mixture of hot tar and stones trialled in 1905 and used widely, with many improvements, thereafter.

ROAD SIGNS AND CYCLISTS

By the 1880s there were around 230 cycling clubs and an estimated 400,000 cyclists in Britain, and this surge in popularity continued with the 'bicycle boom' of 1894–97. However, cycling over rough, unbound surfaces on bicycles with rudimentary brakes could be hazardous, and indeed downright dangerous if steep hills or sharp bends were encountered unexpectedly.

In the late 1870s a few local clubs began to put up roadside notices warning of dangerous descents, a policy eventually followed by various cyclists' organisations, including the Scottish Cyclists' Union and the Bicycle Union, which erected twenty-five danger boards throughout the country in 1879–80. From 1884 the Cyclists' Touring Club (CTC) and the Bicycle Union – by then known as the National Cyclists' Union (NCU) – jointly organised the danger board scheme. The signs read 'To cyclists this hill is dangerous' with NCU and CTC spelled out in full below. The CTC and NCU went their separate ways in 1894,

A National Cyclists' Union warning sign at North Rode, north-east of Congleton (Cheshire), where a narrow lane descends sharply to a main road. The octagonal sign was installed around 1900. The equivalent Cyclists' Touring Club caution sign was rectangular, with black text on a yellow ground. The sign was extant until around 2005, but has been replaced. (Steve Marland)

continuing to erect signs independently, although the CTC was more prolific. Caution signs, for undefined hazards, were introduced in 1897. By 1902, well over 4,000 cyclists' danger and caution signs could be found on roadsides.

SIGNAGE FOR THE MOTOR AGE TO 1964

Motoring organisations soon followed the example of the cyclists, with the Automobile Club (founded 1897) – later the Royal Automobile Club (RAC) – starting to erect caution signs in 1901. During 1903 the club developed diamond-shaped pictogram signs, which were used on the London to Portsmouth road. Excluding the pointing hands of earlier mileposts, this was probably the first use of symbols rather than text for road signage in Britain. Following the Motor Car Act of 1903, implemented in 1904, local authorities became responsible for all traffic signs. They were required to put up warning signs, mainly at steep hills, crossroads and dangerous corners. It was recommended (without any enforcement) that caution should be indicated with a hollow red triangle, prohibition by a solid red disc and speed limits using a white ring with a plate below giving the figure.

Most authorities were less than enthusiastic about installing signs, and as the suggested format was potentially variable, the result was only a slow improvement in overall

The First and Last Inn at Sennen (Cornwall) with its circular AA village nameplate showing distances to Land's End, Penzance and London. It was installed between 1923 and 1932. The inn survives, but minus the AA sign. From a 1930s postcard. (Author's personal collection)

The total solar eclipse of 29 June 1927 was the first seen over the British mainland for 203 years. Millions travelled to watch, congregating on the line of totality between North Wales and the North Sea. Richmond (North Yorkshire) lay at the centre of the zone, a fact marked by the AA with its distinctive yellow sign. (Mark Whyman)

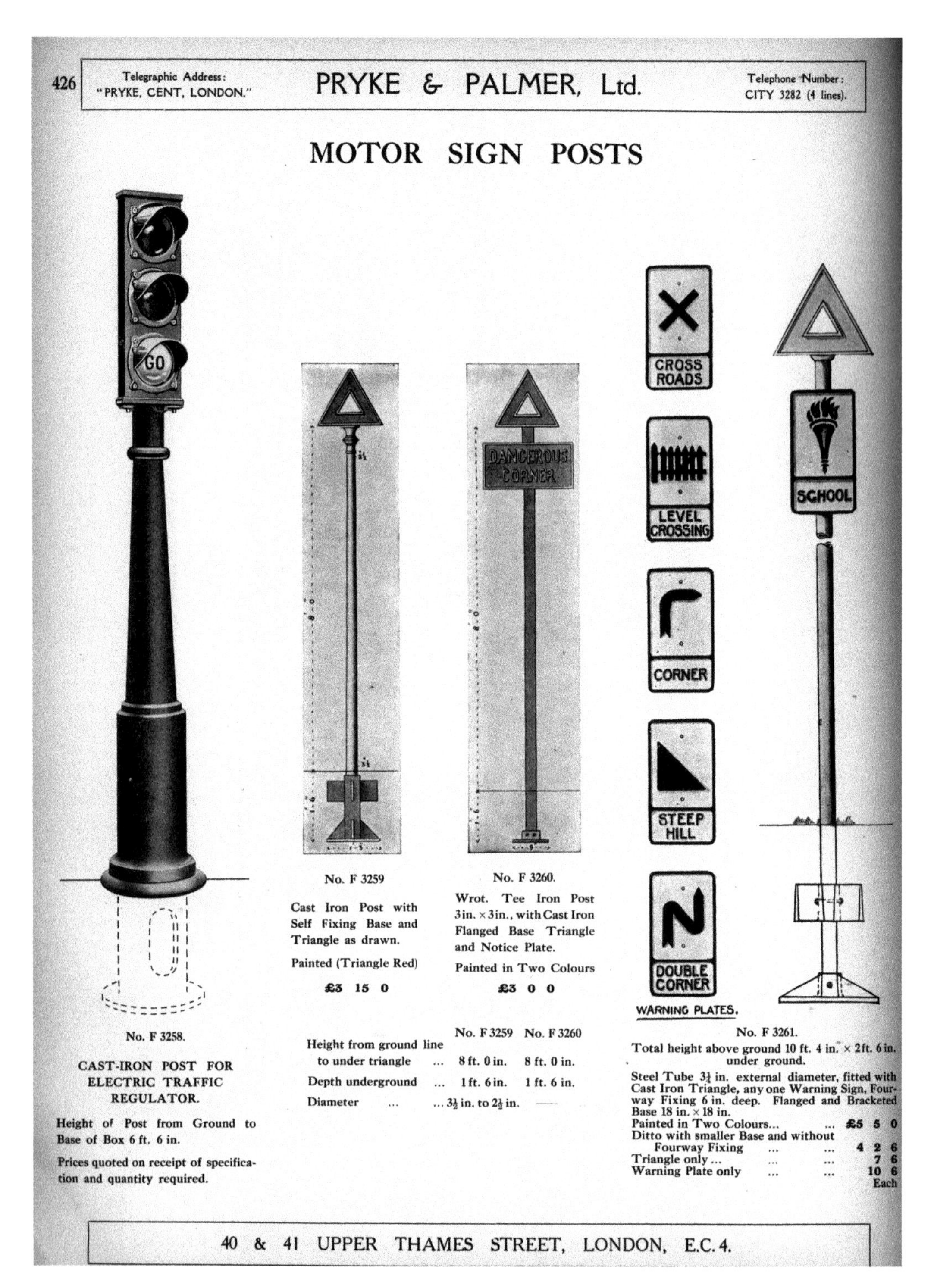

426 Telegraphic Address: "PRYKE, CENT, LONDON." **PRYKE & PALMER, Ltd.** Telephone Number: CITY 3282 (4 lines).

MOTOR SIGN POSTS

No. F 3258.

CAST-IRON POST FOR ELECTRIC TRAFFIC REGULATOR.

Height of Post from Ground to Base of Box 6 ft. 6 in.

Prices quoted on receipt of specification and quantity required.

No. F 3259

Cast Iron Post with Self Fixing Base and Triangle as drawn.

Painted (Triangle Red)

£3 15 0

No. F 3260.

Wrot. Tee Iron Post 3in. × 3in., with Cast Iron Flanged Base Triangle and Notice Plate.

Painted in Two Colours

£3 0 0

	No. F 3259	No. F 3260
Height from ground line to under triangle ...	8 ft. 0 in.	8 ft. 0 in.
Depth underground ...	1 ft. 6 in.	1 ft. 6 in.
Diameter	3½ in. to 2½ in.	—

No. F 3261.

Total height above ground 10 ft. 4 in. × 2ft. 6 in. under ground.

Steel Tube 3¼ in. external diameter, fitted with Cast Iron Triangle, any one Warning Sign, Fourway Fixing 6 in. deep. Flanged and Bracketed Base 18 in. × 18 in.

Painted in Two Colours... ...	£5 5 0
Ditto with smaller Base and without Fourway Fixing	4 2 6
Triangle only	7 6
Warning Plate only	10 6 Each

40 & 41 UPPER THAMES STREET, LONDON, E.C. 4.

Post-1921 pictogram road signs advertised in the huge 1930 trade catalogue issued by general ironmongers and builders' merchants Pryke & Palmer of London. The enterprising firm included a cast-iron post for an electric traffic regulator; traffic lights were introduced only three years before. (Author's personal collection)

provision. There were exceptions: Berkshire County Council, for instance, erected 450 triangular caution signs as well as boards at the entrances to every town and village, requiring drivers to slow down. In response to the general reluctance of local authorities to install new signs, the Automobile Association (AA), formed in 1905, began its own programme of warning and directional signage, which also served to advertise the organisation. By late 1906 signs had been put up on fourteen different roads, and in the following year the AA introduced its distinctive village nameplate. These mostly yellow roundels, around 3 ft (1 m) in diameter, showed the village name in yellow on a black horizontal band, with distances to nearby destinations above and below. Between 1906 and 1939 the AA put up over 30,000 village signs in Britain, but most of them were removed during the Second World War when invasion was perceived to be a threat. Around sixty-five such signs remain in situ today.

In 1921 the recently formed (in 1919) Ministry of Transport brought in a range of recommended rectangular pictogram signs, warning of hazards such as level crossings and double corners. Each cast-iron sign was to be placed on a post below a hollow red triangle, now signifying danger. The number of pictograms was later expanded, and uniform signs finally became a statutory requirement in 1933. Although these 1930s signs were supplanted by a new set of pictograms in the 1960s, a few examples of the old signage can still be found on our roads.

SIGNPOST DEVELOPMENT 1888–1964

When county councils took over responsibility for direction signs in 1888, they inherited an unsystematic collection of signs made of wood, iron, stone or a combination of these materials. The duty of signposting and repairing the main roads was onerous and costly. Hampshire's county surveyor reported in 1894 that the county's 293 posts would need to be supplemented by another 528 posts with 1,652 arms to fully signpost the county, including the through routes to larger towns. At an estimated £2 per post this was no small burden, but some counties, including Gloucestershire (in 1902), did manage to overhaul their entire stock of posts. Designs and materials varied from county to county. In Cornwall, turn-of-the-century signposts were mostly cast iron and made by seven local foundries, all with their own slightly differing designs. The column, which bears the foundry name or mark, is topped by a finial, often pointed, below which the arms are mounted.

The unsatisfactory nature of much signposting was highlighted in 1911 by a committee of interested parties including the county councils and their surveyors, road engineers and the RAC. Its recommendations included iron posts with wooden arms at least 8 ft (2.4 m) above the ground. However, potential legislation was overtaken by the onset of war in 1914, and it was 1921 before a standard design was suggested by the Ministry of Transport. The format was very plain, a white post with arms bearing place names, distances and the newly introduced major road numbers; these were added to existing direction signs where required. Crucially, the responsible authority's identity was also to be specified.

The ministry's model design was adopted by many authorities and the format became mandatory in 1933, with the exception of the post colour, which was modified to black and white bands. Authorities were still able to interpret the regulations with considerable

Above left: A nineteenth-century wood and cast-iron signpost at the west end of Sulham (Berkshire), near Reading, with a recruitment notice pasted to its substantial square post. The village stocks survived until at least the 1920s. From a *c.* 1908 postcard. (Author's personal collection)

Above right: This elegant iron fingerpost (1909) stands on the edge of Fairwater (Cardiff) village green. A cast inscription on the fluted column tells us that it was made in nearby Llandaff by Evans's Eagle Foundry. (Courtesy of No Swan So Fine under CC 4.0)

Above left: An early twentieth-century cast-iron signpost at Shiremoor (North Tyneside), made at Smith, Patterson's Pioneer Foundry in Blaydon (Tyne and Wear). The foundry also produced iron milestones that can still be seen throughout Northumberland. (Lynn Pearson)

Above right: West Runton's is one of twenty-seven surviving original Norfolk village signs, all made by the Royal Label Factory, Stratford-upon-Avon. The flattened-hexagon shape was specified by the Ministry of Transport in 1921. (Courtesy of Kolforn under CC 4.0)

The Pillar of Salt, as this modernist road sign (1935, architect Basil Oliver) is known, stands opposite the remains of St Edmund's Abbey in Bury St Edmunds (Suffolk). The local council wanted a special design for this sensitive site, rather than the standard Ministry of Transport style. (Lynn Pearson)

freedom, resulting in a wide variety of non-standard, locally distinctive signposts appearing during the 1920s and 1930s. The shapes and styles of finials, arms, lettering and to a lesser extent posts all reflected local individuality, and were often the work of local foundries. However, nearly half of them were manufactured at the Royal Label Factory in Stratford-upon-Avon (Warwickshire), established in 1874 to make cast-iron horticultural labels. By the 1930s the firm was supplying not only signposts but road signage of all types. Its cast-iron signposts normally bore the factory's name near the base, and some of these original posts still survive.

During the Second World War many signposts were removed and not reinstated. The 1964 Traffic Signs Regulations stipulated a standard national style for signposts, and local authorities were encouraged to remove traditional fingerposts. The degree of compliance varied. As a result, late nineteenth- and early twentieth-century fingerposts are now relatively scarce, and are more likely to be found in rural areas.

REGULATING TRAFFIC AND CROSSING THE ROAD

Edwardian pedestrians were left to dodge between motor vehicles, horse buses and carriages, trams and bicycles as they made their way across the crowded, mucky streets. A few island refuges were installed on London's streets in 1908, but little more was done to assist those

Traffic control in 1930s Sheffield. The peculiar point duty box is topped by what appears to be a Belisha beacon, while two pedestrians ignore the 'Please cross here' sign – directing them to an island refuge – on the pavement to the left. From a late 1930s postcard. (Author's personal collection)

Three hand-operated petrol pumps outside a High Street garage in Chipping Norton (Oxfordshire) during mid-May 1932. Illuminated pump heads identify the brands available, including Shell and National Benzole. Glass cylinders allowed drivers to see the fuel measured before it entered the vehicle's tank. From a 1930s postcard. (Author's personal collection)

on foot until the 1920s when pedestrian crossings, some with illuminated 'cross now' signs, were introduced. To make crossings more noticeable, Belisha beacons (after the then Minister of Transport, Leslie Hore-Belisha) were placed at the kerbs during the mid-1930s. These 7-ft-high (2.1 m) striped poles topped by unlit orange glass or enamelled sheet steel globes proved controversial and were prone to vandalism. They survived in altered form from 1953 – with illuminated flashing glass globes – to accompany the recently introduced black-and-white striped zebra crossings, and beacons in various styles are still with us today.

Regulating traffic at junctions had always been problematic. Into the 1920s, police spent much time on point duty, standing at junctions directing traffic, and were sometimes sheltered by specially constructed sentry boxes or gazebo-like huts. There were experiments with manual and electric semaphore-style signals to control traffic and crossings, as in Brighton from 1927. Also in 1927, Britain's first automatic electric traffic lights appeared – in Wolverhampton. They were found to be more efficient at controlling traffic flow than police on point duty, and the basic traffic light design remained little changed until the late 1960s, when they were replaced by new lights produced in conjunction with renowned industrial designer David Mellor (1930–2009).

ROAD AND DIRECTION SIGNS FROM 1964

Basic map-style advanced direction signs had been introduced in 1933. These flat, rectangular panels displayed road numbers and place names combined with directional arrows. They were precursors of the signs in use on our larger roads today, which were brought in following the creation of a modular signage system for the new motorways of the late 1950s. The blue motorway signs, with what became known as their 'Transport' typeface in white, were the work of designers Jock Kinneir (1917–94) and Margaret Calvert (b. 1936). The pair went on to produce signs for the remainder of the road network, which became law on 1 January 1965. The warning and information signs were now mainly symbolic; an estimated 1.6 million of the old signs needed to be changed. Directional signs for primary routes had a green background, other routes had white backgrounds, while local destinations were white with a blue border (this ceased in 1994). The original signs were made of sheet metal, but very few have survived. Modern signs are aluminium composites, while the typeface has been digitised. New signs are introduced from time to time; for instance, the small mammal warning sign, featuring a hedgehog within a red triangle, which was launched in 2019.

In the 1970s, the remaining traditional signposts benefitted from an increasing interest in cast-iron street furniture on the part of local authorities, who became more aware of its heritage and community value. In addition, the surviving signposts often needed

This ring junction (1972) in Swindon (Wiltshire) is known as the Magic Roundabout, after the BBC children's TV series (1965–77) of the same name that became a cult hit. Traffic travels clockwise, as normal, round the outer circle and anti-clockwise on the inner circle of five mini-roundabouts. The sign was photographed in 2005. (Courtesy of Dickbauch in public domain)

Some of the road signs introduced in 1965, as shown on the back of a Shell touring map of northern England. They were still described as New British Traffic Signs, although the map was published in 1972. (Author's personal collection)

refurbishment, and from 1994 authorities were once again allowed to install new signs of the old fingerpost type. Suppliers still include the Royal Label Factory, based at Buxton (Derbyshire) as part of Leander Architectural since 1998, among a greatly diminished number of British ironworks.

LIGHTING THE STREETS

In post-medieval London, illuminating night-time streets was the responsibility of individuals rather than the authorities. Householders and some traders were supposed to hang lanterns – initially candles, later oil lamps – outside their premises during the night for at least part of the year. The system was so inefficient that public lighting was introduced in the early eighteenth century, with residents paying a 'lamp rate'. The parish of St Marylebone had 2,500 oil lamps of its own by 1773, numbered for ease of maintenance (just like modern lamp posts).

The first major advance in street lighting came in 1807 with the arrival of gas lamps in Pall Mall. By 1814 there were 22 miles of gas-lit roads in the capital, their lanterns often topping cast-iron columns 13–16 ft (4–5 m) in height. The new technology then spread rapidly throughout Britain, as local authorities often allowed private gas companies to lay their mains (and dig up the roads) only if they provided cheap gas for public lamps. By 1826 nearly all towns with populations over 10,000 were supplied, and by the mid-1840s most towns over 2,500 were lit.

Of course, this presented great opportunities for the manufacturers of iron lamp posts (also variously standards, columns or pillars) and lanterns. Victorian ironfounders such

Dundas House (1774, out of view to the right), Edinburgh, became the Royal Bank of Scotland's headquarters in 1825. Its cast-iron railings (1827) were made locally by Anderson's Leith Walk Foundry, while the splendid gas lamp standards (1828) came from Shotts (north Lanarkshire). The Shotts Iron Company was known worldwide for its decorative lamp standard castings. (Lynn Pearson)

Above left: An elaborate bronze lamp standard on Gloucester Gate Bridge (1877), near London's Regent's Park. The bridge was designed by William Booth Scott (1822–91), chief surveyor to the Vestry of St Pancras. He signed the lamps, which were supplied by lighting specialists Gardner's of the Strand. Their restoration in 2008 required the production of over a hundred bronze castings. (Lynn Pearson)

Above right: For Queen Victoria's 1887 golden jubilee, this 20-ft 6-in (6.2-m) clock tower, with drinking fountain and gas lamps, was erected in Harlesden (London Borough of Brent). The elaborate design came from the catalogue of McDowall, Steven & Co.'s Milton Iron Works in Glasgow (trading as Steven Bros & Co. in London). The tower survives, although minus its lanterns. From a *c.* 1907 postcard. (Author's personal collection)

as Macfarlane's Saracen Foundry of Glasgow offered a wide range of elaborate standards, often with classical ornament. These were complemented by equally ostentatious lanterns, although the four-sided lantern with canted panes was probably the most widely used design. Extra light in the streets came from the huge lamps hung by many shops and pubs above their windows and doorways.

Despite the rise of electricity from the 1880s, gas street lighting continued well into the twentieth century. Steel became the most popular material for columns, although concrete

Lamp standard designs from the 1914 catalogue of engineering firm Ham, Baker & Co., based in Westminster and Langley Green (West Midlands). The dolphin pattern (centre) was a version of the original *c.* 1870 Thames Embankment standards supplied by the Coalbrookdale Company of Ironbridge (Shropshire). (Author's personal collection)

Brixton's Electric Avenue, built in 1885, was one of the first streets in London to be lit by electricity. The lamps hang beneath glazed canopies that sheltered pedestrians and made it such a popular shopping street. From a *c.* 1905 postcard. (Author's personal collection)

London's Piccadilly Circus at night in 1951, showing the effectiveness of its street lights amid the array of neon advertisements. The lights are probably high-wattage tungsten lamps installed in 1931, with American lanterns and cast-iron columns from Mackenzie & Moncur's foundry, Edinburgh. From an early 1950s postcard. (Author's personal collection)

was used from the late 1930s until the mid-1990s. Electric street lights came to the fore between the wars, and many gas lanterns were converted to electricity. Increasing electric road signage, such as traffic lights and Belisha beacons, became a significant new market for the electricity companies. However, it was not until after the Second World War that electricity began to overtake gas for public lighting. Birmingham had 35,000 gas lamps in the 1930s, finally removing its last one in 1975, while London's central boroughs still have around 1,100 functioning gas lamps.

Until the 1950s lantern design was generally based on historical precedents, with manufacturers offering ranges of ornate styles designed for (and by) the authorities that originally commissioned them. Change came about during post-war reconstruction, and later the new town programme when architects such as George Grey Wornum (1888–1957) became involved with the planning of public lighting. Grey Wornum designed an elegant new lighting column and tungsten lamp for Westminster, which proved so successful it remained in production until the 1980s.

A fluorescent street light designed for Cambridge by architect Sir Albert Richardson. A total of 120 were installed during the late 1950s and around half of them survive. Mounted on posts or wall brackets, they became known as Richardson Candles. The design was based on the Festival lamp post manufactured by Revo of Tipton during the 1950s and 1960s. (Courtesy of David Curran in public domain)

The weighbridge in Rothesay (Isle of Bute) and its late nineteenth-century former weighing house, which held the scale connected to the balance in the pit beneath the iron plate. Beside it is one of the traditionally styled lamp posts, bearing the arms of the Royal Burgh of Rothesay, installed in 1995 to match the extant Victorian originals. (Lynn Pearson)

Birmingham's public lighting department joined the Revo electric company of Tipton (West Midlands) to produce lights celebrating the 1951 Festival of Britain. The result was the Festival, a cast-iron classical column topped by a tall fluorescent lantern, which sold well during the 1950s and 1960s. David Mellor's minimalist tubular steel lighting columns, designed for the engineering firm Abacus of Sutton-in-Ashfield (Nottinghamshire), were also popular from the mid-1950s. In the 1960s sodium lamps on columns of concrete or tubular steel became commonplace, although concrete was being phased out by the 1980s.

The UK's current stock of 6 million or so lamp posts includes everything from nineteenth-century gas lamps to the latest in energy-efficient LED (light-emitting diode) installations. Increasing numbers of traditionally styled lamp posts are being introduced, designed with and for local authorities to fit into environmentally sensitive areas and add to local identity.

AROUND OUR STREETS

There is much more to look out for in and around our streets. Bollards – initially wood, then iron – have been used since the eighteenth century to control traffic. Similarly, corner stones (known as bumpers or glinters in some areas) of iron or stone protected buildings from passing carriage wheels; iron examples sometimes carry the maker's name. Internally lit bollards first appeared between the wars – normally on traffic islands and carrying 'keep left' or other notices. Around 1938 Revo of Tipton produced art deco designs for illuminated cast-iron warning pillars, as they were then termed.

Georgian and Victorian terraced housing was often divided from the street by iron railings, which could be extremely elaborate. From the mid-nineteenth century they were normally cast iron rather than more expensive wrought iron. The catalogues of ironfounders contained many hundreds of alternative designs, and railings sometimes bore the maker's name. Many railings were dismantled during the Second World War for recycling at ironworks and as an aid to employment. There were complaints about the chaotic and damaging removal process, but it appears most of the railings were eventually reused. However, several Scottish islands did not lose their railings, and the streetscape of Stornoway (Western Isles) is now a reminder of how our streets once looked. Also close to the highway are street names, little pieces of history, whether simply painted onto buildings or carefully designed signage.

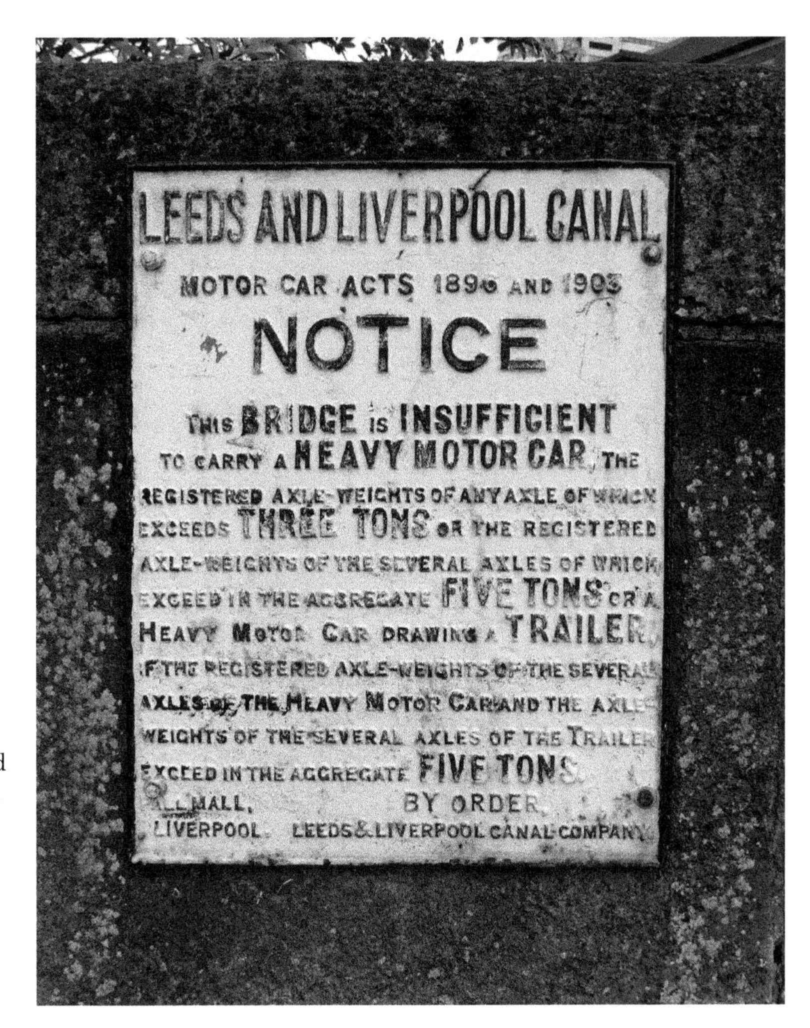

An early twentieth-century statutory sign warning heavy vehicles not to cross the bridge over the Leeds and Liverpool Canal at Wharf Approach, Leeds. Most canal bridges were built at a time when traffic was all horse drawn. (Lynn Pearson)

An unmanned, manually operated railway level crossing at Cambois (Northumberland). The metal gates, with their red 'targets', are opened and closed by a signaller or other rail staff when required. The UK has around 1,500 level crossings on public highways, mostly with automatic barriers. The number of legacy crossings like Cambois is dwindling. (Stephen Veitch)

A Staffordshire blue paving brick, celebrating the ascent to the throne of George V in 1910, set just above a pavement in Wolverton (Milton Keynes). Commemorative bricks were often made on royal occasions like jubilees and weddings, but few remain in street locations. (Lynn Pearson)

Cast-iron railings at a house in Stornoway (Western Isles). The much-overpainted maker's name – Macfarlane's – can be seen on the side of the bottom rail. This design appeared in the sixth edition of the Saracen Foundry's catalogue towards the end of the nineteenth century, along with well over a thousand other patterns. (Lynn Pearson)

A car, probably a Bristol-made Straker-Squire, parked next to a set of fine cast-iron railings around 1910. Today iron railings are often painted black, but in the eighteenth century a cream or stone colour was the norm, while the Victorians preferred green, dark blue, red and chocolate brown. From an early 1900s postcard. (Author's personal collection)

These weighty quatrefoil iron gate piers and railings stand at the gateway to the former Literary and Scientific Institute (1859, now a youth hostel) in Coalbrookdale, Shropshire. The Coalbrookdale Company, whose nearby foundry cast the ironwork, funded the institute's construction. The bronze war memorial (1919) now commemorates those who fell in both First and Second World Wars. (Lynn Pearson)

In Bungay (Suffolk), at least thirty-two street name signs bearing the date '1919' were cast by the local Rumsby's ironworks as an act of remembrance for those who died in the First World War, most of which remain in place today.

Other street furniture includes public seating, with Victorian specimens normally the most ornate. Few benches can match the 1870s array on London's Embankment with their cast-iron sphinx and camel arms. Boundary markers – of estates, parishes, cities, counties, railway companies and more – in streets (and further afield) range from architecturally elaborate stone columns to easily missed pavement inserts. Decorative village signs date

Above left: The surviving upper part of a London & North Western Railway boundary post in Marsden (West Yorkshire). A complete cast-iron tombstone-type post would protrude 2–3 ft (0.6–0.9 m) above ground. Boundary marker designs varied between companies. They were used where fences were impractical or the company's land extended well beyond fenced rail tracks. (Lynn Pearson)

Above right: A Royal Arsenal Co-operative Society (RACS) boundary marker, probably dating from around 1905, in the pavement outside a Co-op store in Eltham (Greenwich). Such stones defined the edge of RACS property available for expansion. (Lynn Pearson)

Bedfordshire marked the 1951 Festival of Britain with the production of new signs, including the Festival logo, for most of its towns and villages. Many survive and most have been refurbished, including this example in the hamlet of Wingfield, but the supports at least appear to be original. (Lynn Pearson)

back to 1912 but rose in popularity after the Second World War, adding to the local sense of place. There are now more than a thousand in England – mostly in Norfolk and Suffolk.

Litter bins, developed from 1925, were the focus of much design effort up to the 1960s, although many were removed in the 1980s and 1990s due to IRA bomb threats. Parking meters, rather like clocks on stalks with a coin slot for payment, were introduced to Westminster in 1958. Pavements lined with meters, one for each space, soon proliferated, but the early years of the twenty-first century saw them replaced by anonymous payment cabinets covering numerous spaces, or even dispensed with altogether in favour of phone payment.

Collection boxes for maritime charities have long been a feature of our seafront promenades. Most commonly seen today are the roughly 4-ft-diameter (1.2 m) spherical, steel sea (naval) mines repurposed as red and white collection boxes by the Shipwrecked Mariners' Society. The mines were donated to the society after the Second World War, and

A montage of Ordnance Survey marks made when mapping Britain before the advent of satellite technology. Bottom right is the most common, a traditionally cut benchmark with a bolt-cut benchmark above. Left is a flush bracket, around 6 in (0.15 m) high, used at more important sites. Around 500,000 benchmarks were created, many in roadside locations on buildings. (Lynn Pearson)

around sixty of them can be seen along the UK coastline. More rare are Royal National Lifeboat Institution (RNLI) octagonal cast-iron pedestals, with coin slots in their domed caps. Probably designed in the early 1900s, they were made by Preston & Bishop's Victory Foundry in Birmingham and are still being installed between the wars. The strangest RNLI collecting box must be the 1886 painted cast-iron sculpture of a cod at Robin Hood's Bay (North Yorkshire). It may be the oldest RNLI box still in service. The fish stands around 4 ft (1.2 m) high, accepting donations through its mouth.

Above: A former RNLI standard design collection box, around 3 ft 3 in (1 m) high, on Bexhill seafront (East Sussex), which was installed in 1935. Further street-side examples remain in Aldeburgh (Suffolk), Weston-super-Mare (Somerset), Clovelly (Devon) and Porthgwarra (Cornwall), while others are in RNLI collections. (Courtesy of Dr-Mx in public domain)

Left: Dog-shaped collection boxes for charities including the Royal Society for the Prevention of Cruelty to Animals (RSPCA) and the Guide Dogs for the Blind Association were popular from the 1950s to the 1970s. Several survive on today's streets; this RSPCA dog is just off the Market Square in Stow-on-the-Wold (Gloucesterhire). (Alena.K/Bigstock.com)

2

WATER AND POWER

Most medieval towns obtained their water from wells or springs, although some built piped or conduit systems – conduits were gravity-powered channels usually carrying spring water. People obtained the water at conduit heads (often known simply as conduits), which contained lead water tanks. Though relatively small, conduits were substantial and sometimes elaborate structures; London boasted sixteen of them by the end of the sixteenth century. Surviving stone-built conduits include two in Lincolnshire: at Lincoln, dating from around 1540, and Grantham (1597).

This landmark iron water tower (1870) served the Great Western Railway works in Swindon (Wiltshire). Before 1980, when a glass-reinforced plastic tank replaced the larger original cast-iron tank, it was one of a handful of all-iron water towers left in Britain. (Lynn Pearson)

London first had a regular pumped water supply in 1582 when the London Bridge Waterworks provided a limited amount of rather impure water from the Thames to four outlets. The New River Company was a much larger concern, bringing spring water from Hertfordshire to the growing city via a canal built in 1609–13. These undertakings were the antecedents of modern-day water companies.

Most people in London and elsewhere continued to get their water from wells, pumps, conduits and rainwater butts until the latter part of the nineteenth century. It was an expensive and time-consuming business, as many of these operations were private and charged for water, as did itinerant water sellers. Some manufacturers with their own sources offered free water to their workers and families.

The mid-nineteenth century saw the establishment of many more water supply undertakings, including public and private companies, and local authorities. They built networks of pumping stations and water towers, with pressurised water mains running beneath the streets. By 1910 there were 2,160 water suppliers in England and Wales, but many of the earlier pumps remained a viable source of water for domestic use until well into the twentieth century.

WATER PUMPS

Over 5,000 free-standing, hand-powered water pumps are thought to survive in the UK, the majority of them in England. Dating from the eighteenth century onward and often made of cast iron, they exhibit an enjoyable variety of design, although many are relatively plain.

London's late eighteenth-century Aldgate Pump, at the junction of Leadenhall and Fenchurch Streets, seen in 1874. Its 5-ft-high (1.5 m), wrought-iron gas lantern fitting was removed in the early 1900s, but a specially made replica was installed in 2019. The landmark pump marks the start of London's East End. (Wellcome Collection. Attribution 4.0 International (CC BY 4.0))

Above: The Market Place pump in Southwold (Suffolk) was presented to the town by its mayor in 1873 and still survives. Made locally at Child's foundry, it features a spout in the form of a herring with three more herrings at the apex of its triangular shaft, their tails supporting a spherical lamp. (Author's personal collection)

Right: The original village pump in Hemyock (Devon) was quite a small affair. It was replaced in 1902 with this wonderfully ornate, cast-iron structure combining water pump, well head and street light, commemorating the reign of Queen Victoria and the coronation of Edward VII. Note the jumble of signage to the rear. (Courtesy of Nilfanion under CC 4.0)

Some occupy prominent positions as focal points on village greens or marketplaces, while others remain significant urban landmarks. A few were combined with drinking troughs, milestones, boundary markers or similar items, and several were installed to celebrate events such as the jubilee of a monarch. Some pumps were housed in open-sided, normally timber-framed shelters, which could be quite elaborate; a few had thatched roofs and some were stone-built. Such is their local importance that water pumps were frequently renovated as millennium projects around 2000.

Occasionally, pumps were in such noteworthy locations that an architect became involved. On Cornhill (City of London) is a pump in the form of a tall cast-iron obelisk, erected in 1799 on the site of a well first used in the thirteenth century. Funded by the Bank of England and local firms including fire insurers and the East India Company, this was a high-profile project needing a reliable designer. The man chosen was builder-cum-architect Nathaniel Wright, who was also district surveyor for the northern part of the City of London. The pump was made by Southwark ironfounders Phillips & Hopwood, and restored in 2013.

Cast-iron pumps were manufactured by numerous ironfounders based throughout the UK. One of the most successful concerns was Joseph Evans & Sons of Wolverhampton (West Midlands), which functioned between 1810 and the mid-1960s; its 1897 catalogue included over 300 different pumps. Hydrants – outlet pipes with valves for pressurised water – were also supplied by many pump makers, and indeed resembled pumps without handles. Several late nineteenth-century examples survive, often fluted iron columns with domed caps.

DRINKING FOUNTAINS AND HORSE TROUGHS

In the mid-nineteenth century, the inadequate public supply of clean water became a matter of concern to the industrial and political classes, initially in the north of England. Unable to afford piped water, poorer people relied on often polluted wells and pumps, the only alternatives being beer and gin. Charles Pierre Melly (1829–88), a Liverpool merchant and philanthropist, took the notion of drinking fountains from those he saw in Geneva during 1852. He then paid for the installation of a series of fountains in Liverpool. The first was erected in 1854, and by 1858 there were more than thirty, nine of which survive. The most common design, in polished red granite, was a simple mural fountain (one built into or attached to a wall): a vertical slab held a spout above a projecting basin, to which two drinking cups were attached.

Other towns and cities, many in northern England, soon followed Melly's initiative, with funding coming from individual benefactors and local authorities. London began to catch up with the reforming zeal of the north in 1859, when the Metropolitan Free Drinking Fountain Association (MFDFA) was founded. A philanthropic, evangelical and pro-temperance organisation, its first fountain opened on 21 April 1859 and by 1861 eighty-five had been installed, although not all local officials were enthusiastic about providing a water supply. The fountains were heavily used but also subject to vandalism.

In 1867 the association began to provide troughs for animals, altering its name to the Metropolitan Drinking Fountain and Cattle Trough Association (MDFCTA). Not only was

Above left: A cast-iron 1850s drinking fountain funded by Charles Pierre Melly in the extensive wall of the former Clarence Dock, north of Liverpool's centre. A spout in the shell-shaped arch delivered water, to be collected in a cup suspended on a chain (now missing). (Courtesy of Phil Nash under CC 4.0)

Above right: Still mostly intact, the Queen Victoria fountain was one of six drinking fountains installed in Bristol during 1859. Donated by a local philanthropist, it was designed by London sculptors the brothers W. J. & T. Wills for the Coalbrookdale Company foundry in Shropshire. Their cast-iron surround was a stock item that appeared in the Coalbrookdale catalogue. (Courtesy of 14GTR under CC 4.0)

water essential to horse transport, but this change of focus allowed the association to call on the financial support of the animal welfare lobby. The MDFCTA was the most prolific of the charitable organisations providing troughs throughout Britain, building 633 by 1886. Most of them were straightforward designs in granite, often bearing inscriptions, although some bath-like, cast-iron troughs were also installed.

Drinking fountain design soon progressed from inexpensive mural fountains to lavishly ornamented freestanding compositions. The surge of interest in fountain provision was accompanied by design competitions reported in the architectural press, and the MDFCTA itself commissioned architects and sculptors. Ironfounders also offered a wide choice, from plain to heavily ornamented with naturalistic flora and fauna. The end result was an enormous variety of styles, forms, materials and elaboration. Donors, whether through the MDFCTA or acting individually, also had a considerable stake in designs, many of which fulfilled a commemorative or memorial role.

Left: This London fountain was the first erected by the Metropolitan Free Drinking Fountain Association. It opened on 21 April 1859 but was moved in 1867 during the construction of Holborn Viaduct, losing its elaborate arched stone surround. The fountain was later reinstated in the railings of St Sepulchre's Churchyard. Note the drinking cups. (Courtesy of Acabashi under CC 4.0)

Below: A combined horse trough, dog trough and drinking fountain seen in use on the village green at Pembury (Kent), soon after it opened on 31 July 1909. It was provided by the MDFCTA in memory of local Protestant martyr Margery Polley, who burned at the stake in 1555. The trough is extant, but now functions as a planter. From a *c.* 1910 postcard. (Author's personal collection)

The 27-ft (8.2-m) public drinking fountain (1867) in Dudley marketplace (West Midlands) remains one of the most elaborate in the country. Designed by sculptor James Forsyth and donated by the Earl of Dudley, it appeared in *The Builder* of 7 March 1868. Forsyth previously carved the enormous *Perseus and Andromeda* fountain at the earl's residence, Witley Court. (Look and Learn)

Two similar drinking fountains at Middleton-in-Teesdale (Durham) and Nenthead (Cumbria), were presented in 1877 by London Lead Company agent R. W. Bainbridge. George Smith & Co.'s Sun Foundry, Glasgow, made both. Shown here is Middleton, with crocodile detailing symbolising the purity of the water. (Mark Whyman)

Above left: The Queen Victoria drinking fountain (1897) in Fort Augustus (Highland), at the south end of Loch Ness. Its design was based on a standard item in Macfarlane's Saracen Foundry catalogue, specially adapted for the diamond jubilee with the queen's image. Note the salamanders, symbolising courage, near the pedestal base. (Lynn Pearson)

Above right: The Alexandra Fountain was erected by William Longair to commemorate visits made by Queen Alexandra to Dundee in 1907 and 1908, while he was Lord Provost of the city. It stands beside the Tay, near Discovery Point, a little way west of its original position. Its classical form is topped by a handsome pink granite crown finial. (Lynn Pearson)

By 1960 the MDFCTA had erected nearly 2,000 drinking fountains in London (of which around 800 then remained) and around 400 further afield, as well as over 900 troughs. Adding in those put up by other providers, the total countrywide could easily have topped 3,000 fountains. Today, there are more than 700 drinking fountains in the British Isles listed by government heritage bodies for their special architectural and historic significance. Many more unlisted fountains and troughs still make positive contributions to our streetscapes.

DRAINAGE AND SEWERAGE PROVISION

Before sewers were introduced, drainage of waste water and effluents was mainly by natural streams. Early nineteenth-century sewers (underground channels) were built solely for rainwater, but from the 1840s several larger towns and cities began to construct sewerage networks to collect domestic soil and wastewater. In Liverpool, 86 miles (138 km) of sewers were laid between 1848 and 1859, while a scheme in Leeds was completed during 1850 to 1855. Many sewers ran beneath main roads, so these large-scale works often caused great upheaval. London's massive drainage network, built in 1859 to 1875, included several new highways as well as 1,300 miles (2,090 km) of sewers.

In terms of street furniture, sewers are generally out of sight, apart from ubiquitous roadside drain covers (gully grates), manhole covers and the now much rarer sewer ventilation columns. Typically, a nineteenth- to early twentieth-century cast-iron gully grate measured 16 in by 8 in (400 mm by 200 mm), although could be larger. Their main interest lies in the foundry and local authority names often seen on the castings; some also bear dates. Openings normally ran horizontally or vertically (with eight or ten slots), but by 1914 a design with slightly curving, diagonal inclined bars became available. In theory, this was less liable to become choked with leaves and other detritus. Although many older grates have been replaced, enough remain to make studying the gutters a fruitful exercise in local history. Sheffield's earliest in situ grate, for example, dates from the 1830s.

Sewer ventilation columns, also known as stench pipes or stink poles, were once commonplace but have been rendered unnecessary by modern plumbing. Mostly made from cast iron (but occasionally brick), their purpose was to ventilate the sewer system, removing unpleasant and potentially harmful fumes. The tall, hollow cast-iron pipes resembled lamp posts without lanterns, and many suppliers sold columns that could be used either for lighting or as stink pipes. Normally there was some minor decorative feature at the top of the column.

A montage of Webb's sewer gas destructor lamps seen around Seaton Delaval (Northumberland). The base of the cast-iron post bears details of Webb's company and his patent. At the nearby seaside, in Whitley Bay and Monkseaton (both North Tyneside), seventeen Webb lamps were erected in 1900 to 1910, of which ten survive. (Lynn Pearson)

Nineteenth-century vent pipes survive in locations including Liverpool, Wolverhampton (West Midlands), Bideford and Plymouth (both Devon), but the most extravagant specimens were erected in Carshalton (London) as part of the 1896–1903 sewerage installation designed by eminent sanitation engineer Baldwin Latham (1836–1917). The vent pipes, of which around twenty-eight remain from the original infrastructure scheme, were made by Macfarlane's Saracen Foundry. The columns were topped by a strange arrangement of ironwork fittings with an ornate arrow at its base, then a vented globe beneath a coronet, and finally a spiked finial.

A more complex method of removing fumes from sewers was invented by Joseph Edmund Webb (1861–1936), whose sewer gas destructor lamps were installed widely throughout England and Wales during the early twentieth century. Webb's destructor lamps were gas lamps (fed from the mains), which were connected to the sewer. The updraft caused by burning gas drew the noxious fumes up the shaft, acting as a vent. In Sheffield, where the city's hills often caused sewer gas to be trapped, eighty-four Webb lamps were erected and around twenty-five remain. They were also popular with seaside authorities, which could not afford a reputation for bad smells.

PUBLIC CONVENIENCES

Public urinals erected by municipal authorities first appeared in Britain during the 1820s. Prefabricated cast-iron urinals were put up in Glasgow from the late 1840s onward, with Macfarlane's Saracen Foundry supplying a significant number during the 1850s.

Macfarlane's Saracen Foundry, Glasgow, issued the sixth edition of its catalogue around 1882–85, and the near-700 pages remained valid during the 1890s. The range of urinals was limited, but their elements could be varied to suit specific locations. (Author's personal collection)

Their numbers continued to grow from the mid-nineteenth century onward. Both London and Glasgow had almost 200 by 1875, most of those being able to accommodate several people.

Macfarlane's urinal designs were heavily patterned, and other manufacturers followed this lead. The Glasgow firms McDowall, Steven & Co., George Smith & Co.'s Sun Foundry, and the Lion Foundry of Kirkintilloch – around 6 miles (10 km) north of the city – successfully promoted their urinals to local authorities nationwide via their illustrated catalogues. Typically, the structures were rectangular in plan, usually roofless and often painted green (rather like the colour of today's broadband cabinets). However, lavishly ornamented circular designs also featured, some with street lamps mounted above the domed urinal. Larger models were available for locations such as tram termini where crowds might be expected.

By the 1880s several thousand cast-iron urinals must have been dotted around Britain's towns and cities, but they were far from popular due to their very obvious presence as reminders of public urination. Norwich (Norfolk), for instance, built few urinals because of objections from local residents and businesses. The solution found here was to erect architecturally sensitive designs to blend in with existing buildings. More generally, in the 1890s local authorities began to remove existing urinals and build new facilities, often underground. Only a few cast-iron urinals survived this process, and the further losses in

Above left: This cast-iron urinal (probably 1880s) with floral and Adam-influenced decoration stands outside the Jewellery Quarter station in Birmingham. It was made by James Allan Senior & Son's Elmbank Foundry, Glasgow. Six of the city's seven other surviving urinals were also supplied by Allan, in varying sizes but the same style. (Courtesy of Brianboru100 under CC 4.0)

Above right: A knapped flint and terracotta circular public urinal (1902) in Norwich (Norfolk) by A. E. Collins, city engineer in 1898–1925. It stands in a sensitive situation, close to fifteenth-century St Andrew's Hall. (Courtesy of Iridescent under CC 4.0)

wartime. Birmingham still has at least eight cast-iron urinals, including the elaborately roofed (if rather battered) example in Balsall Heath. Others are extant in Bristol and London, as well as at open-air museums, heritage railways and similar spots.

Although water closets (WCs) were invented as far back as the 1770s, public provision was almost completely lacking. The Society of Arts, organisers of the 1851 Great Exhibition, asked the Metropolitan Commission of Sewers to supply more public facilities in London's streets ahead of the exhibition, but little was forthcoming aside from some elegantly drawn plans. Thus, it transpired that our first popular public conveniences were provided at the exhibition itself. Pioneering sanitary engineer and toilet manufacturer George Jennings (1810–82) installed a series of simplified WCs that were used by both men and women a total of 827,820 times.

The City of London then allowed Jennings to build the world's first underground public conveniences in 1855; the site was in front of the Royal Exchange. No more were erected

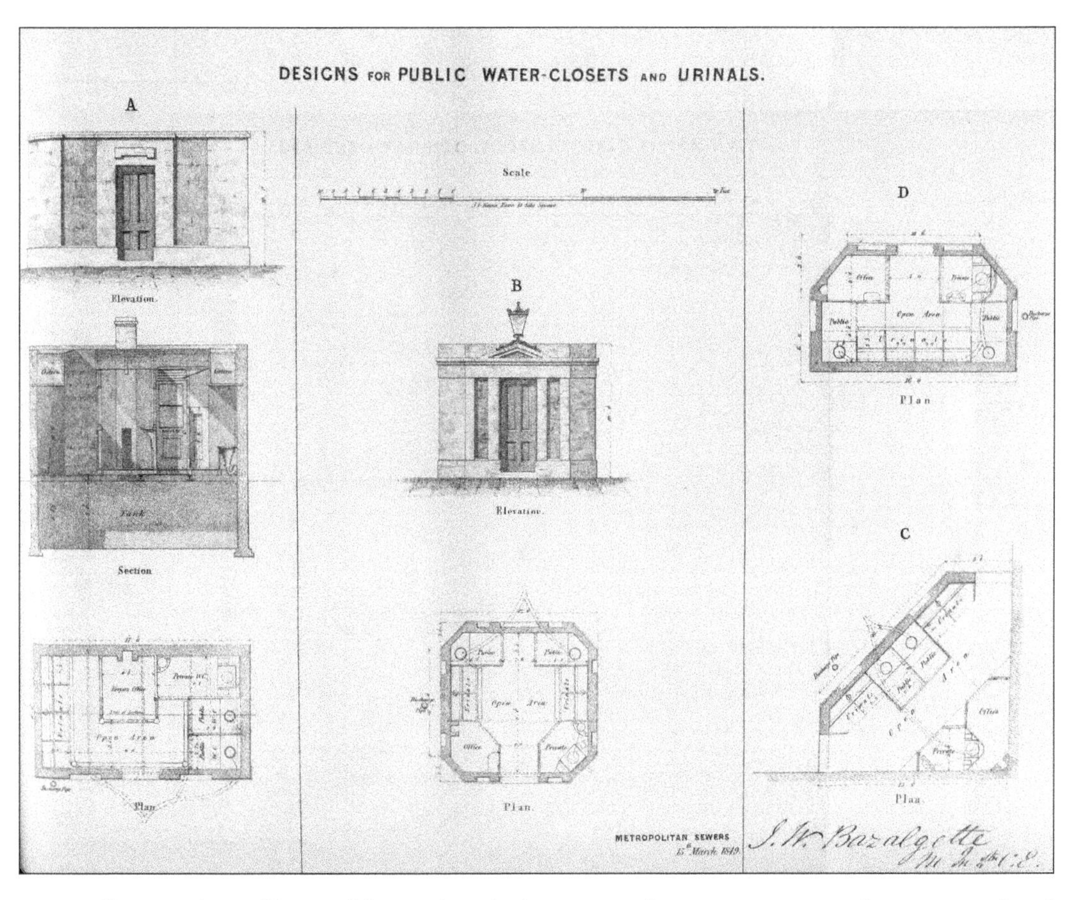

Following the Public Health Act (1848), the Metropolitan Commission of Sewers produced a series of plans during 1848 to 1851 for public toilet facilities in London. The engineer Joseph Bazalgette, appointed assistant surveyor to the commission on 16 August 1849, signed this plan for classical-style water closets (prepared several months earlier), as he began to take responsibility for public convenience design. (Wellcome Collection. Attribution 4.0 International (CC BY 4.0))

until the late 1880s, when suddenly the underground loo (with its urinals and WCs) became a fashionable alternative to above-ground urinals. By 1895 thirty-six British towns and cities could boast public conveniences – mostly underground and for men only. The City of London then had fifteen underground loos, but only one catered for women as well as men. London's most elaborate underground facility was at Piccadilly Circus, where the lavatories opened in 1889 (for men and women) were signalled in the street by bold ironwork lamps from the Saracen Foundry; the loos survived until the 1920s. Glasgow's first underground toilet opened in 1892, following the removal of an existing urinal on the site.

Although the bulk of the structure was underground, public conveniences could still be significant landmarks, and were frequently sited on traffic islands or other intersections. A tall ironwork ventilation pipe, usually fitted with a lantern, was the most visible element, along with decorative iron railings and gates marking out the stairs. The ensemble was often completed by a set of iron bollards. The ground above the loos was often fitted with pavement lights, that is iron frames containing small rectangular or circular sections of glass, which lit the space below; the frames were strong enough to take normal pedestrian

A modern view over the former men's underground public conveniences erected at Newcastle upon Tyne's Bigg Market in 1898. The circular structure held eighteen urinals and five cubicles, reached via a steep, winding stair and sheltered under a metal-framed glass roof. The building closed in 2012, then reopened in February 2020 as a wine bar. (Lynn Pearson)

Hull's Market Place *c.* 1912. On the central island are the gilded statue of William III with its late nineteenth-century lamps, and beyond it a cabmen's office. In between come the railings and roof of the underground gentlemen's public conveniences (1901–06). Sanitary engineers B. Finch & Co. of Lambeth supplied the lavish interior. From an early twentieth-century postcard. (Author's personal collection)

The underground public conveniences at London's major New Cross Gate junction (Lewisham) were installed in 1897 by sanitary engineer George Jennings for the local Board of Works. The central gas lamp-cum-ventilation pipe, as well as the handsome cast-iron bollards, were from Macfarlane's Saracen Foundry. The tram shelter, constructed around the lamp standard, was added in 1911. (London Metropolitan Archives, City of London; Collage: the London Picture Archive, Ref. 232064)

Left: Eminent Scottish architect Alexander 'Greek' Thomson designed cast-iron ventilating pipes at New Cross Gate (seen here) and just east at Clifton Rise (both Lewisham). Thomson's column appeared in Macfarlane's catalogue, along with its base, by Glasgow architect James Sellars. The two 1897 columns, both moved a short distance after their public conveniences were demolished, are thought to be the sole works in England by Thomson. (Lynn Pearson)

Below: An illustration from the *c.* 1929 catalogue issued by Haywards Ltd of Southwark, manufacturers of pavement lights, showing how effectively their products could illuminate underground public conveniences. (Collection of Ian Macky)

traffic. Inside, the walls were normally glazed brick or tiles, and the floor mosaic or terrazzo. The range of equipment could be lavish, with expensive ceramic, marble and teak fittings.

The vogue for underground facilities petered out early in the twentieth century. A number of complete examples survive, and several have been converted into arts or hospitality venues. Others remain intact, but locked and disused; they pose clear difficulties for accessibility. Of course, construction of above-ground facilities continued into the twentieth century, with an emphasis on greater provision for women and higher architectural quality. A rare surviving example of an early women-only toilet was built in Berwick-upon-Tweed (Northumberland) in 1899. The pretty little half-timbered rustic cottage is reminiscent of contemporary sports pavilions, many of which provided facilities for women spectators.

Between the wars, public conveniences were often provided at transport hubs: railway stations, bus or tram stops and termini, and the occasional ferry landing. Architecturally they were a varied bunch, encompassing Edwardian and neo-Georgian styles along with art nouveau and art deco features. One of the most unusual is the ten-sided precast concrete urinal (1919) in Norwich, designed by the city engineer Arthur Elliston Collins (1857–1933), who had a special interest in concrete. Its sides bear highly ornate patterns, probably a

The West Pier public conveniences (1899–1900) in Rothesay (Isle of Bute). Visiting gents could use fourteen Adamant urinals by Twyfords of Hanley (Staffordshire) (note the cistern above) plus the central hexagonal urinal range. The dark dressing round the urinals, which Twyfords called St Anne's Marble, is a transfer printed ceramic product. This is one of Britain's most elaborate and luxurious loos. (Lynn Pearson)

Above: Decorative detailing from the public conveniences (1926) in Hull (East Yorkshire) that served a tram stop for the nearby Humber ferry, replacing an old cast-iron urinal. An early example of toilets designed for ladies and gentlemen, the mostly intact interior features sanitary ware by Duckett's of Burnley (Lancashire). (Courtesy of Notafly under CC 4.0)

Left: The flatiron-style Westbourne Grove public toilets (1991–93, Piers Gough) for ladies and gents in London's Notting Hill incorporate a small shop and a large public clock. The building is clad in specially made glazed bricks from Ibstock Brick. Close by are a drinking fountain (MDFCTA, 1900) and a granite horse trough (2006) erected by the local Pembridge Association. (Lynn Pearson)

reference to the city's similar but lost 1880s cast-iron (or possibly precast concrete) urinals. When built, the urinal stood in a busy industrial area, close to the former Norwich City railway station and a tram line. It is now probably England's oldest precast concrete urinal. The material became more popular in the 1920s, but designs were normally much plainer.

Relatively modern toilets worth seeking out include the glass-canopied, turquoise wedge of loos (1991–93, architect Piers Gough) in London's Notting Hill and the sharply geometric concrete block (2007, Plastik Architects) at Gravesend (Kent). However, the latter, a landmark structure intended to aid the area's regeneration, is currently closed. It fared better than the striking modernist toilets in dark blue brick erected at Accrington (Lancashire) in 1968. Designed by borough architect Raymond Duckworth, the block was demolished by 2002.

POWER

The gas industry's main contribution to our stock of street furniture is the gas lamp, but on a much larger scale, now-obsolete iron gasholder frames (gasometers) from the nineteenth and early twentieth centuries should also be considered. Originally commonplace, these feats of engineering still dominate townscapes due to their height, which can reach around 100 ft (30 m). Gasholders were tanks containing water and a circular iron vessel, the bell, that held the gas. The bell rose or fell as the gas volume varied, thus the misleading term gasometer. Larger gasholders had telescopic bells with two to four sections. Elegant, architecturally

The Gas Light & Coke Company built this distinctively classical gasholder frame (1883) at its St Pancras gasworks in London. Relocated northward, minus its bell and tank, it encloses Gasholder Park, near King's Cross station. At the base of each cast-iron column is the roller carriage, which moved the bell up and down the column's guide rails. Three adjoining frames from the same gasworks now surround apartments. (Lynn Pearson)

elaborate guide columns and skeleton-like frames, usually wrought or cast iron, held the bell in place. Many of the hundreds once in use have been demolished, although a few have been incorporated into housing and other developments, as in Dublin and London.

Evidence of early electricity distribution undertakings is still visible in our pavements. On Tyneside, a pioneering area for electric power, the Newcastle upon Tyne Electricity Supply Co. (known as NESCo) set up a substantial power supply network in the early twentieth century. Residents in the city's affluent suburbs of Jesmond and Gosforth were targeted, and NESCo access covers for power cable ducts can still be seen set into local pavements. Incised hieroglyphic marks on nearby kerbstones indicated which houses were supplied and the presence of cable joints, junction boxes and the like. Electricity access covers related to the networks of private companies and municipal authorities can be found elsewhere in Britain, along with a variety of kerbside markings probably made by workers from power companies or other utilities.

Access covers installed by the Newcastle upon Tyne Electricity Supply Co. (NESCo) set into a pavement in the Newcastle suburb of Jesmond. NESCo, formed in 1889, became a significant supplier in the early twentieth century. It was a world leader in power station development during 1900–30. (Lynn Pearson)

A montage of six kerbstones from Gosforth, Newcastle upon Tyne, showing early twentieth-century incised NESCo symbols. The street appears above the kerb in all photographs, and most of the arrows point towards specific houses. These hieroglyphs are the antecedents of spray paint markings used by modern utilities. (Lynn Pearson)

Small roadside cabinets containing electrical equipment (for local supply, street lights and tramways) were common features of early twentieth-century power networks. Generally, around 3 ft (0.9 m) in height with a little decoration, the majority were made by William Lucy's Eagle Foundry in Jericho, Oxford, which sold them throughout the country from the 1890s until the 1960s. They bear the foundry mark 'Lucy Oxford' and have become known as Lucy boxes. Many still remain in the north-west of England, the more recent cabinets being almost devoid of ornament.

A rarer element of early power-related street furniture is the transformer pillar, a type of substation. The oldest known to survive is an elaborate, square cross-section cast-iron structure made by Macfarlane's Saracen Foundry, installed in the centre of Derby around 1893. Only slightly more common are those produced at the start of the twentieth century by the British Electric Transformer Company of Hayes (then Middlesex, now Hillingdon),

Above left: Universally known as 'Lucy boxes' after the Oxford foundry that cast many of them, this ornate cabinet on the seafront at Llandudno (Clwyd) was actually made by Hardy & Padmore's Worcester foundry, which advertised a similarly decorative design in 1921. It may have held electrical equipment for the adjacent tramway. (JohnDavid/Bigstock.com)

Above right: One of the two British Electric Transformer Company (BETC) pillars surviving in Newport (Gwent). This example, which unusually supports a lamp column, stands next to an old sewer vent pipe. Only five other BETC pillars are known to be extant: two each in Sheffield and Surrey, and one in Wimbledon (London). (Courtesy of No Swan So Fine under CC 4.0)

which manufactured highly ornate cast-iron cylinders to house transformers. Stamped with the firm's name, they stood around 8 ft (2.5 m) high. Several local authorities bought these transformer pillars, but only five remain in England and two in Wales; perhaps more may be discovered. There are also a few held by industrial museums. Another example, in Audenshaw (Greater Manchester), was shattered by a car in June 2020, showing the vulnerability of our historic street furniture.

The national grid transmission system became established between the wars, and the electricity industry was nationalised in 1948 (only to be de-nationalised in the 1990s). In Europe, many substations continued to be housed in metal columns (often used for advertising), but in Britain they usually took the form of small, rather blank-faced buildings that often pass unnoticed. Since the 1960s there have been a few examples of definite architectural interest, such as Sheffield's brutalist Moore Street (1965–68), and others disguised as artworks.

In the centre of London's Elephant and Castle (Southwark) roundabout is a memorial (1960–61, architect Rodney Gordon) to physicist Michael Faraday (1791–1867), who was born nearby. The rectangular structure is clad in stainless steel and encloses a Transport for London transformer substation. (Lynn Pearson)

A Transport for London substation, visible from Edgware Road (Circle Line) Tube station and adjoining roads, hides behind *Wrapper* (2012), a colourful art installation by Jacqueline Poncelet. Covering more than 1,800 sq yds (1,500 sq m), it is the largest vitreous enamel artwork in Europe. The patterns, which reflect elements of the locality, were screen printed on to over 700 sheet steel panels. (Lynn Pearson)

3

COMMUNICATIONS AND TRANSPORT

THE LETTER BOX

The postal reforms of 1840 made sending a letter relatively cheap and easy, using the new adhesive stamps to prepay postage. The main drawback was that mail still had to be taken to the nearest receiving office until the General Post Office (GPO, established in 1660) eventually considered adopting a system of roadside letter (or post) boxes, similar to those already found in Europe. The first four British letter boxes appeared during 1852 in St Helier, Jersey (Channel Islands). These prototype red-painted, cast-iron pillar boxes were hexagonal and around 4 ft (1.2 m) high; they were cast at a local foundry. Three more were installed early the following year at St Peter Port, Guernsey, where one still remains in use.

The experiment was such a success that it was extended to the mainland in September 1853. There was no standard letter box, as each GPO district surveyor was responsible for design in their own area, and many different foundries were involved. Generally, however, the new pillar boxes were octagonal with a vertical aperture or slit (unlike the 1852–53 prototypes) and painted dark green. The oldest survivor from this period still in public service is thought to be the 1853 postbox at Barnes Cross, Holwell (Dorset), made at John Butt's Gloucester foundry.

Letter box design evolved by trial and error during the 1850s, with costs and formats varying greatly. An elegant circular, fluted specimen was produced by ironfounders Smith & Hawkes of Birmingham's Eagle Foundry during 1856 to 1857, and eight of these are still in service. In 1859 the GPO decided to standardise its pillar boxes, settling on a design that incorporated the best features of previous boxes. Available in two sizes for nationwide use, the cylindrical National Standard box had its horizontal aperture located beneath a protective cap to combat the weather.

The standard box was functional but rather dull, and other designs were soon being installed, including the elaborate hexagonal model known as a Penfold – named after its designer, Surrey architect John Wornham Penfold (1828–1909). In use from 1866, around 300 Penfolds were manufactured over a thirteen-year period, and more than a hundred

Above left: Only eight of the elegant, fluted postboxes made in 1856 to 1857 by Birmingham firm Smith & Hawkes are still in service. Note the vertical letter slot. This one stands in Oxton, Birkenhead (Merseyside). (Courtesy of Spudgun67 under CC 4.0)

Above right: A larger variation of the 1859 National Standard letter box was developed in Liverpool around 1863 to cater for the city's high volume of mail. Seven Liverpool Specials, topped by a cast-iron crown, were made by Cochrane & Co. of Dudley (West Midlands). Only one survives in service, near the Albert Dock (not its original location). (Courtesy of Steve Knight in public domain)

Left: A Victorian Penfold letter box, painted its original green, in the High Street at Rochester (Kent). From 1988 the Post Office introduced replica Penfolds at some historic and tourist sites. (Courtesy of Ethan Doyle White under CC 4.0)

remain in use. Initially they were green, but from 1874 letter boxes were painted bright red – pillar box red – to increase visibility.

The iconic cylindrical pillar box was introduced in 1879 and continued to be the basic box design until the late 1960s. Early versions, produced in 1879 to 1887, omitted the royal insignia, but from 1887 all boxes have born the cypher of the current monarch. However, in Scotland the EIIR cypher is replaced by the Scottish crown, as the present queen is not Queen Elizabeth II of Scotland. A new rectangular steel pillar box was introduced in 1968 to speed up the clearing of letters, but was found to corrode quickly; it was replaced in 1974 by a cast-iron version. More striking was the modernistic 1981 K-type, a cast-iron cylinder with an integral top produced initially by the Lion Foundry at Kirkintilloch. Its smooth

Above left: This Edward VII red pillar box is the classic cylindrical design used from 1879 onward, albeit with the larger door and integral aperture introduced from 1904 to aid clearing the box. The ironfounder's name, displayed on the base, is McDowall, Steven & Co., London and Glasgow. (Lynn Pearson)

Above right: Oval letter boxes with dual apertures, for local and other mail, were introduced in 1899. This example, at Moreton (Merseyside) on the Wirral, displays the EIIR cypher and bears one of the increasingly rare Post Office direction signs. The box was made by the Lion Foundry of Kirkintilloch. (Courtesy of Phil Nash under CC 4.0)

Above left: A K-type letter box produced during 1981 to 2001. This one was supplied by Abbot Engineering of Paisley (Renfrewshire). Its new features included a rotating disc showing numbers of the next collection. Each number became visible through a small window in the collection times plate, which has disappeared from this box. (Lynn Pearson)

Above right: From 1881 wall boxes were supplied by architectural ironfounders W. T. Allen of London, whose name appears at the base, although they were actually made at the Sherwood Iron Foundry, Mansfield (Nottinghamshire). This Victorian box is the smallest of the four sizes produced – 28 in by 10 in (711 mm by 254 mm). (Lynn Pearson)

lines did not please everyone and the old cylindrical boxes were brought back in 1990. Production of the K-type ceased in 2001.

Over 60 per cent of British postboxes carry the EIIR cypher or the Scottish crown, while around 15 per cent date from the reign of George V (1910–36). Numbers then diminish in the order George VI, Victoria, Edward VII and finally Edward VIII, with 138 working pillar boxes surviving from his brief 1936 reign. Although the red pillar box is instantly recognisable, over the years since 1879 there have been many small changes in the elements that make up the design. Variants of the royal cypher, aperture size and placement, door size, collection times plate, shape and design of the cap, and presence or otherwise of the contractor's name are just a few of the features that can be altered. In total, there are around 800 different types of postbox.

Small rectangular boxes suitable for fitting into existing walls were introduced in 1857 and manufactured until 1980. Many sub-post offices had wall boxes supplied by James Ludlow of Birmingham. Originally, these were partly faced with a black and white enamel plate carrying the royal cypher and the words 'Post Office Letter Box'. Known as Ludlow boxes, over 5,000 were produced between the mid-1880s and 1965, but fewer than 300 remain in service as sub-post offices are increasingly shut down. Another design of small postbox, first used in London during 1896, was intended to be attached to a lamp post or

Above left: This unusual, round-topped Edward VII wall box, designed to be attached to a lamp post, was originally used solely for collections from the home of eminent Newcastle upon Tyne resident Cecil A. Cochrane, of the extensive ironfounding family. The box, cast by Handyside's of Derby, was later repurposed for deliveries. (Lynn Pearson)

Above right: A letter box at Kirkby in Ashfield (Nottinghamshire), resplendent in newly applied gold paint in honour of local swimmer Ollie Hynd, 2012 Paralympic gold medallist. The box itself dates from before 1991, when 'Royal Mail' replaced 'Post Office' below the royal cypher. (Courtesy of Dan Sellers under CC 4.0)

One of sixteen post boxes in central Dublin rainbowed (vinyl-wrapped) by Ireland's postal service An Post during the city's 2019 Pride Festival. Following independence in 1922, Irish post boxes were painted green; from 1939 the Department of Posts and Telegraphs 'P&T' also began to appear, as on this example. (Courtesy of Smirkybec under CC 4.0)

other pole. They were often installed in rural areas where the amount of mail was low, and can also be used as wall boxes or mounted on pedestals.

Currently there are over 85,000 roadside letter boxes in England alone, and around 115,500 in the UK. Recent years have seen a number of boxes decorated to mark events including the 2012 Summer Olympics and Paralympics (gold), Christmas 2018 (white snowflakes) and the 2019 ICC Cricket World Cup (blue). In spring 2020, during the Covid-19 pandemic, boxes outside some major hospitals were painted NHS blue, with 'Thank You NHS' in white lettering. October 2020 saw four boxes given a new livery of black with gold trim for Black History Month.

PUBLIC TELEPHONE BOXES

Telephones began to appear in Britain during the late 1870s. Initially they were used for private point-to-point communications, until several independent companies started to provide telephone exchanges, allowing a customer to contact any other customer in discrete geographical areas. From 1884 the companies were permitted to build trunk lines, connecting towns and cities, and to set up public call offices, giving wider public access to the telephone network. They were normally located in railway stations, shops, hotels and the like. By 1886 seventy-five call offices had been installed, including the first freestanding call offices (or kiosks).

Above left: A K1 Mark 235 kiosk (1922), topped by a telephone sign and wrought-iron finial, outside the sub-post office at Taverham (Norfolk). The signage differentiates it from the first national kiosk design (K1 Mark 234), which had minimal signage and a pyramidal roof. Note the sub-post office's Ludlow letter box, below its small window. From a mid-1930s postcard. (Author's personal collection)

Above right: This unique telephone box is Giles Gilbert Scott's timber prototype K2, his winning entry in the 1924 standard kiosk design competition. Following judging, the kiosk was moved to Burlington House on London's Piccadilly. It stands west of the entrance gateway, complementing a cast-iron K2 on the east side. Note the pierced lettering; the production model had painted lettering. (Lynn Pearson)

Each company came up with its own design, but generally call offices were basic, sentry box-like huts with a closing door, holding just a single caller and the telephone equipment. The most common designs were wooden, like tiny garden sheds. In East Anglia, the Norwich type of call office had a simple pitched roof, while the Birmingham pattern, used for Midlands call offices, was topped by a pavilion roof, sloping on all four sides. Of course, there were other possibilities: an ornate, domed, hexagonal cast-iron call office (looking rather like a pissoir) operated in Holborn (London), a tiny octagonal call office functioned in Bolton (Greater Manchester) from 1905, while a picturesque rustic cabin appeared at the tram terminus in Blackburn (Lancashire) in 1907. The rustic, branchy style often featured in transport-related buildings around the turn of the century. The National Telephone Company alone was running 7,800 call offices by 1907.

Eventually the telephone service was nationalised, with the GPO taking control of most exchanges in 1912 – Hull, East Yorkshire, was one exception. Moves to standardise call offices were thwarted by the onset of war in 1914, although some preliminary designs for a national kiosk had already been prepared by the GPO, based on the Birmingham model. The new kiosk, known as K1 Mark 234, finally arrived in 1921. It was a square cross-section, half-glazed cubicle with a pyramidal roof, built from precast concrete panels with a wooden door; normally it was painted white with a red door.

However, the K1 was seen as outdated from the start, and was installed mostly in rural locations. It was modified in 1922, but efforts to find a replacement resulted in the Royal Fine Art Commission holding a competition in 1924, from which the neoclassical K2 design by eminent architect Giles Gilbert Scott (1880–1960) emerged. Larger than the K1, constructed in cast iron with a teak door, it was expensive and heavy, making it unsuitable to employ nationwide. The K2 was the first of the iconic red phone boxes, and around 1,700 of them were installed by 1934, mostly in London; well over 200 survive.

While Scott was coming up with a more cost-effective design for national use, the K1 series soldiered on in the form of a third version, the K1 Mark 236, with increased glazing. It was produced between 1927 and 1929. Altogether, around 6,300 examples of the K1 range were originally erected in the UK, but only seven are known to survive – all in England. The sole kiosk in a roadside location is at Bembridge in the Isle of Wight; the others are mostly at museums or other heritage sites. Two more remain in Ireland: one currently in store, the other – in Irish cream and green livery – on the main street in the centre of Foxrock, south Dublin.

Scott's new K3 was introduced in 1929 and became the standard GPO kiosk until 1936. A simplified and smaller version of the K2, it was constructed from concrete panels with a teak door and the paintwork was white with red glazing bars. Although around 11,000 K3s

A replica K1 Mark 236 telephone kiosk, with distinctive three-quarter-length glazing, at the ghost village of Tyneham (Dorset), evacuated during the Second World War. The villagers never returned, but there is now limited public access. Tyneham's original K1 Mark 236 was installed in 1929 but lost during the 1980s. The replica was completed in 2012. (Lynn Pearson)

Above left: The sole example of Giles Gilbert Scott's K3 design to survive in a roadside location, outside the former post office at Rhynd, near Perth. Just in view on the left is a Elizabeth II post box bearing the Scottish crown. (Red Box Archive/Alamy Stock Photo)

Above right: The K4 kiosk-cum-post box in Whitley Bay (North Tyneside) is one of three still in roadside locations, although the lamp above the postal side is missing. Only fifty K4s were produced, as finding suitable sites proved difficult due to their inconvenient size. The 1932 experimental oval pillar box incorporating a stamp vending machine was more successful, with around twenty-two surviving on our streets from the 125 boxes cast. (Lynn Pearson)

were once in use, they are now very rare, with only a single example still in a roadside location, at Rhynd near Perth.

In the 1930s the GPO experimented with an enlarged version of the K2 that also carried a letter box and two stamp machines on its rear side. This huge phone box was the K4, made by the Carron Company of Falkirk. Up to fifty of the cast-iron monsters were installed, during 1930 to 1935, and eleven are known to remain in Britain – all in England. Just three of these occupy roadside locations, in Whitley Bay (North Tyneside), Frodsham and Warrington (both Cheshire). Another contemporary experiment was the mysterious K5, a 1933–34 GPO prototype for a smaller, simpler kiosk that never saw the light of day.

The GPO again commissioned Giles Gilbert Scott to design a truly national kiosk to commemorate the silver jubilee of George V in 1935. Scott's K6, the best known of the red phone boxes, was a K3-sized version of the K2, rather plainer and modified for mass

Above: An imposing row of K6 telephone kiosks, Giles Gilbert Scott's classic 1935 design, in central Preston (Lancashire). Around 2,500 K6s, including these nine, are listed by official UK heritage bodies for their special architectural and historic interest. (Courtesy of Francis Franklin under CC 4.0)

Left: Hull Corporation (Hull City Council from 1972) bought the city's telephone network in 1914, soon after the GPO took over most other exchanges. Hull's kiosks are all painted creamy-white and do not bear the royal crown. This K8, seen in 2015, has since been removed but Hull still has the UK's largest K8 cluster, with five. (Courtesy of Alex Liivet in Public Domain)

production. Over 65,000 K6s were manufactured, mostly at four Scottish foundries, between 1936 and 1968 – around 11,000 remain. In the 1960s the GPO began to search for a more modern kiosk and selected a design by the respected architect Neville Conder. Prototypes of the K7, a glass and aluminium cubicle, appeared in 1962, but the weather proved too much for the new kiosk and the project went no further.

Instead, architect Bruce Martin (1917–2015) produced the elegantly engineered K8, the last in the line of red phone boxes. He drastically reduced the number of components and replaced the small panes of glass with large sheets. It was made of cast iron with an aluminium door, while the roof bore illuminated panels reading 'Telephone'. Between 1968 and 1983 around 11,000 K8s were made for the Post Office, mostly by the Lion Foundry of Kirkintilloch. Under forty survive, with only eighteen in roadside locations.

The privatised concern British Telecom (BT from 1991) was created in 1984, taking over Post Office telecommunications business. In 1985 it began to replace the existing stock of kiosks with the new KX series of lightweight phone boxes. The most widely installed was the flat-roofed, shower-cabinet-like KX100, succeeded in 1996 by the KX100 Plus, with its red domed roof. Other companies, including Mercury Communications (1988–94) and New World Payphones (from 1996), also began to provide public phone facilities. However, as mobile phones increased in popularity, usage of phone boxes decreased dramatically. From a peak of 137,000 BT kiosks in 1999 the number dropped to 46,000 in 2017, with around 8,000 being classic red telephone boxes.

New World Payphones (established 1991) installed its first new kiosk, made by Dorset sheet metal fabricators MVM, in 1996 and were operating around 1,200 public telephones in the UK by 1999. These two kiosks, with folding doors, are MVM1000s; the later MVM7000 has a single door. Behind the kiosks are early twentieth-century art nouveau, wrought-iron spear railings. (Lynn Pearson)

The rise of the mobile phone, along with broadband technology, added a great deal of clutter to our crowded streets. Mobile phone antennas are sometimes embedded in road signs, or their masts disguised as trees. The 5G network, currently being rolled out, requires taller monopoles (around twice the height of a typical lamp post) and more cabinets at its base than previous iterations. The appearance and exact function of the now ubiquitous roadside broadband cabinets varies according to network provider. Openreach (for BT) uses dark green steel cabinets, rectangular boxes around waist height with angled tops; older BT cabinets were cast iron, and a few are still in service. Recent Virgin Media cabinets are normally a silvery grey, but older boxes may also be green. CityFibre cabinets are olive green. Occasionally some cabinets are transformed into artworks, as at Kelham Island (Sheffield) where specially decorated boxes became part of an arts and heritage trail in 2019.

POLICE BOXES

The city of Glasgow police began to experiment with telephone communication in 1880, and in 1891 introduced police boxes with telephones on to the city's streets, enabling officers on the beat and the police station to contact one another. The box was a fabulously ornate hexagonal, cast-iron structure topped by a huge gas lamp, which lit up when the station needed to speak to an officer. The boxes were manufactured locally by Macfarlane's Saracen Foundry, and indeed resembled their pissoir designs. By 1914, fifty-six of the red-painted boxes were in use.

A police box in Newcastle's Bigg Market, with a gentlemen's circular underground public toilet (1898) to the rear, from the 1928 *Police Journal.* The telephone was also available for public use to summon emergency services. This design was first used in Sunderland, where the local department store Binns supplied the boxes. (Author's personal collection)

Above: Outside Sheffield's town hall stands the sole survivor of 120 police boxes introduced to the city by its chief constable, Percy Sillitoe, from 1928. A small door beneath its window hides a public telephone. The timber box has a gently arched roof, in contrast to the later London police box with its pyramidal roof. (Tupungato/Bigstock.com)

Right: A former police telephone box standing in its original location on Sandside, beside the harbour at Scarborough (North Yorkshire). The wooden box, really a miniature police station, was probably designed locally and dates from the late 1920s or 1930s. (Courtesy of Simon Reinhardt under CC 4.0)

Above left: In 1937 G. M. Trench, creator of London's police boxes, designed the police pillar, housing a public telephone. The 7-ft (2.1-m) cast-iron posts were intended for narrow streets. Nine survive, including this light blue City of London Police example near St Paul's Cathedral. The GPO's police pillar, with a triangular head, had been introduced in 1932. (Courtesy of Ethan Doyle White under CC 4.0)

Above right: The former police box near Waverley station, Edinburgh, is now a café. The city's classically detailed police boxes, designed in 1931 to 1933 and originally a dull blue colour, were a little larger than London's square boxes and rectangular in plan. The windows have saltire-shaped glazing. (Lynn Pearson)

Despite the success of the Glasgow system, it took until the 1920s for something similar to be adopted in England. Frederick James Crawley (1880–1966), chief constable of the Sunderland and River Wear force, pioneered the English police box in an attempt to increase the efficiency of his officers. Sunderland's twenty-two green-painted wooden police boxes, introduced in 1923, were inexpensive and resembled early public call offices. Crawley became chief constable of neighbouring Newcastle in 1925, and police boxes soon appeared throughout the city. Forces in other areas including Reading (Berkshire), St Albans (Hertfordshire), Coventry (West Midlands), Huddersfield (West Yorkshire) and Manchester then followed suit with slightly differing designs. In Sheffield, Chief Constable Percy Sillitoe – inspired by a visit to the north-east – brought in a total of 120 boxes from 1928 onward, each crowned by a blue electric lamp. A few of these provincial boxes still survive in roadside locations, including one in Sheffield.

The Metropolitan Police introduced their own version to London in 1929. The square, reinforced-concrete box, 9 ft 4 in (2.9 m) high, was designed by the force's architect,

Gilbert Mackenzie Trench (1885–1979), and around 685 were installed. The blue London police box eventually became familiar nationally as the model for the TARDIS in the BBC's *Doctor Who* series, which began in 1963. None remain on London's streets, but four of Glasgow's red boxes, adapted from the London design and installed during 1932 to 1938 as part of the city's 323-box network, are still extant; some are now painted blue. Other forces also used similar concrete police boxes; for instance, Newport (Gwent) had a four-box system, of which one remains.

Edinburgh chose cast iron for its 142 sentry-box-style police boxes, which were designed in 1931–33 by the city architects' department, under Ebenezer MacRae, specifically to complement Edinburgh's classical architecture. They were made at the Carron Company's ironworks near Falkirk. Possibly as many as sixty may survive; certainly over twenty are now listed buildings, making this the greatest concentration of UK roadside police boxes to survive the move to personal radio communication in the 1960s. London's last box was removed in 1981.

MOTORING ORGANISATION PHONE BOXES

The Automobile Association (AA) erected the first shelters for its uniformed patrolmen in 1912, soon equipping the boxes with telephones. At this time cars were notoriously unreliable and members often needed assistance from a patrol. Each AA box, a black timber sentry box with pitched roof and yellow AA signage, eventually had a unique number. There were sixty-one boxes in place by 1920, when members were issued with

An AA patrolman and AA box 52 at the gateway to Sandown Park racecourse (Surrey), on the busy A3 London–Portsmouth road. An original black sentry box design, with stable door and gable-mounted AA sign, it was erected before 1920. After the A3 was realigned during the 1920s the box was moved to the A3/Kingston bypass junction. From an early twentieth-century postcard. (Author's personal collection)

Above: The 68-ft-high (21 m) Clarkson Memorial (1880–81, architect George Gilbert Scott), to a local anti-slavery campaigner, dominates the centre of Wisbech (Cambridgeshire). Before it stands a signpost showing road numbers (introduced 1921). Its black and white post became mandatory in 1933. Note the RAC patrolman on point duty (left) and his RAC box, a pre-1930 Hudlass design. From a 1930s postcard. (Author's personal collection)

Left: Adding the final touches during repainting of AA box 817 at Beadnell, Northumberland, in August 2020. This design of box, with a full-length door, appeared from 1956. The Beadnell box was probably installed during the early 1960s. (Lynn Pearson)

keys. Royal Automobile Club (RAC) boxes could also be seen at the roadside, whose royal blue sentry boxes were designed by RAC consulting engineer Felix Hudlass. These were slowly replaced after 1930 by a flat-roofed, square box designed with the input of noted architect (and Rolls-Royce enthusiast) Edwin Lutyens. By 1938 the AA had installed 637 boxes, but ten years later the RAC still had only 550.

The standard AA box design was reworked several times, with the (now) most familiar version – the cross-gabled black box with yellow trim and winged AA sign – being produced from 1956 until 1967 when the AA reached its peak of 787 boxes in use. At this point the boxes were rebranded with the AA's new square logo, although the winged badge returned in the 1990s. Mobile phone technology finally made the boxes unnecessary. Of the thousand or so boxes installed by the AA and the RAC, probably only eighteen remain in their original roadside locations – all AA boxes and most listed as historic landmarks. There are eight in England, seven in Scotland and three, one listed as recently as 2020, in Wales. Perhaps more remain to be discovered. Failing that, examples of both varieties can be found in museums and heritage locations.

CABMEN'S SHELTERS

The hackney cab, a two- or four-wheeled horse-drawn carriage, was a Victorian antecedent of the modern taxi. By 1890 there were around 12,000 hackney cabs in London and well over 600 public cab ranks, where cabmen waited for custom. Cabs were not allowed to be

This cabmen's shelter, a shed on wheels, was installed at the south end of St Giles, Oxford, in 1876, but does not survive. Nearby underground gentlemen's toilets (1895, awaiting new use) have railings by Oxford foundry Lucys. A cottage-style cabmen's shelter (1896), designed by local builder S. Hutchins, was relocated near this site and is now a food outlet. From a *c.* 1905 postcard. (Author's personal collection)

Left: The cottage-style former cabmen's shelter (1911) at Ripon (North Yorkshire) – the wheels are not original. It came from Norwich prefabricators Boulton & Paul. Their 1898 catalogue included a less ornate shelter, which was supplied 'in sections, ready for easy erection by purchaser'. (Courtesy of Richard Collier under CC 4.0)

Below: The Notting Hill shelter (1909) erected by London's Cabmen's Shelter Fund (CSF). It lacks the hipped roof and decorative dormers of the classic 1882 shelter design, by CSF architect Maximilian Clarke. The shelters generally occupy exposed sites, near or in the middle of busy roads. (Lynn Pearson)

left unattended, but in practice cabmen occasionally tired of being outside in unpleasant weather and retreated to the pub. This was a problem countrywide and attempts were made to raise funds – often from temperance supporters – for shelters to be erected near ranks.

England's first cabmen's shelter was put up in Manchester in 1862. It was a single-storey wooden shed with a sloping roof protruding forward over external seating; inside was a stove and room for perhaps six or seven cabmen. Liverpool, Glasgow and Birmingham soon followed suit with shelters of improved design. A much more decorative shelter was erected in Bradford during 1877. It was designed by T. H. & F. Healey, best known as ecclesiastical architects, and the plan was published by *Building News* in 1878. The rectangular, timber shelter measured 15 ft (4.6 m) by 8 ft (2.4 m) wide, had ornate fenestration and a pitched roof with a ventilator. The single internal space was entered through double doors on the long side. The shelter was moved to Crich Tramway Village (Derbyshire) in 1972, and restored during 2020.

Similar cottage-style shelters were built throughout Britain around the turn of the century. Only a few remain on roadside sites outside London, including those in Oxford (1896), Hitchin (Hertfordshire, *c.* 1910) and Ripon (North Yorkshire, 1911). The largest surviving cluster of cabmen's shelters results from the work of London's Cabmen's Shelter Fund (CSF), established in 1875. Its best-known design is the iconic green wooden hut, with a hipped roof and ornate dormers, that appeared from 1882. Externally, it was very similar to the Bradford shelter, but split internally into a galley kitchen and cabmen's mess room. The CSF built sixty-one shelters during 1875 to 1950 and only thirteen remain, all in central London and most dating from 1888 to 1915; they are still in use by taxi cab drivers.

A few cab shelters were built after the First World War. There are two London examples: the Wharrie shelter (Elizabeth Scott, 1935) is a modernist shed on Rosslyn Hill with a fine mosaic floor panel; it replaced an earlier shelter on the same site. More recently, H-B Designs was responsible for the green, timber-framed shelter erected at Ealing Broadway in 2012.

TRAM SHELTERS

The Tramways Act of 1870 empowered local authorities to licence companies to build and operate tramways. In addition, the tramway route itself could be constructed by an authority and then leased. Horse tramways began to appear countrywide, although the system was problematic as it allowed authorities to terminate licences after twenty-one years (and every seven years thereafter) without proper compensation. This discouraged companies from investing in infrastructure such as tram shelters. Eventually, some municipal authorities began to operate their own tramways, the first being Huddersfield (West Yorkshire) in 1883.

Many routes were electrified from the 1890s onward, and the 'golden age' of trams lasted until the 1930s when motor buses began to replace them. Several tram shelters, perhaps up to forty, survive from the turn of the century and particularly interwar periods, most of them erected by local authorities. Bristol's tram company, which ran the city's extensive network between 1875 and 1937, built no shelters, although its pretty

An unusual survival from London's tram network is the northern portal of Kingsway tram subway (1904–06), seen soon after opening. Note the lack of overhead wires; the sub-surface electric power supply is picked up via a central conduit. The tracks, conduit and granite setts still remain, along with much ironwork including a gas lamp standard. From a *c.* 1908 postcard. (Author's personal collection)

This timber-framed octagonal shelter (1896) is the sole survivor from those lining Huddersfield Corporation's tramway route through the prosperous suburb of Edgerton. It originally had a door. Now serving as a bus shelter, it is painted in the corporation's colours. Little octagonal shelters were popular as they offered good visibility and weather protection, but their footprint was small. (Lynn Pearson)

On significant sites, more ornate structures might be erected, as in the centre of Darwen (Lancashire), where its tramways department erected these two stone-built octagonal shelters (1902) following electrification of the network. The design was by borough engineer Robert W. Smith-Saville (1865–1915). A memorial to the South African War stands between the pavilions. (Lynn Pearson)

Matlock's cable tramway opened in 1893 to take visitors and their baggage up the steep hill to the town's spa hotels. The cable ran in a channel below and between the tracks. The elaborate tram shelter (1899) had stained-glass windows and brass fittings. What remains of it now stands in a nearby park. From a *c.* 1900 postcard. (Author's personal collection)

Extensive tram shelters on Old Haymarket in central Liverpool during the 1920s, with St John's Gardens to the rear. The iron and glass cantilevered shelters are close to public facilities (lower left) including a K1 Mark 234 telephone kiosk and an octagonal tram ticket/enquiries office. Steps leading to underground toilets are also visible. From a 1920s postcard. (Author's personal collection)

Brighton's Old Steine tram shelter (now café), designed in the borough engineer's department under David Edwards (1878–1947; in post 1924–41), was opened in May 1937. Alterations to the moderne shelter meant the loss of some glazing and most of its underground public toilets. Also by the department are three nearby *c.* 1950 bus shelters in similar style. (Courtesy of The Voice of Hassocks in public domain)

octagonal booking offices were similar to many early shelters. One of the most lavish and unusual is Battlefield Rest (1914–15, Frank Burnet & Boston) in Glasgow, a linked pair of octagonal towers clad in green and white faience stripes; the building was restored in 1993 to 1994.

Ornate tram shelters were more common in seaside resorts and other tourist destinations; for instance, the cable tramway shelter (1899) in Matlock (Derbyshire) and the circular, mostly iron and glass shelter (1907) at Llandudno (Clwyd), both of which survive. Shelters in the rustic style appeared at Blackpool and Laxey (Isle of Man), where they were partly tourist attractions. Numerous iron and glass shelters were provided by ironfounders, notably the Lion Foundry of Kirkintilloch. These firms could supply a kit of parts for anything from a simple screen and canopy (a cantilevered shelter) to large, elaborate structures. A substantial 1920s Lion Foundry shelter survives in Portsmouth (Hampshire). A few art deco and moderne shelters also went up in the interwar years: in Blackpool, Brighton and especially Leicester, where five concrete art deco shelters (1934) remain in the suburbs.

BUS SHELTERS

Motor buses grew more common in urban areas during the first decade of the twentieth century. In 1903, Eastbourne Corporation (East Sussex) became the first authority in Britain to run its own bus service. An early shelter, supplied by Norwich prefabricated building manufacturers Boulton & Paul (who also sold cabmen's shelters), survives north of Eastbourne's centre.

Fixed stopping points for buses gradually won acceptance between the wars when cast-iron shelters of various sizes were widely available. An elegant ironwork shelter, still in service in the Plungington area of Preston (Lancashire), may date from this period. Its cantilevered design saves space on the pavement but leaves passengers vulnerable to the weather. In the mid-1930s the London Passenger Transport Board (known as London Transport) introduced sleek modernist designs for bus stops and shelters, including the concrete bus stop posts designed by architect F. R. S. Yorke.

Following the Second World War, several memorial bus shelters were erected in the south of England, such as the delightful, thatched examples at Osmington (Dorset) and Dunchurch (Warwickshire), both still in use. Precast concrete and cast-iron shelters were still available, but the main thrust of 1950s shelter design was towards lightweight, easily assembled structures. The combination of aluminium alloys, glass and concrete was useful in cities; Manchester's 180-ft-long (55 m) shelter in the city centre, erected in 1957, could accommodate 300 people. It was designed by the city architect, Leonard C. Howitt. David Mellor's classic steel and glass shelters were produced from 1956 by the Nottinghamshire firm Abacus. Well over 140,000 were sold, and they could be seen throughout the UK in the 1950s and 1960s.

Bus shelters changed dramatically when they became vehicles for advertising. Two rival companies, Adshel (beginning in Leeds during the early 1970s) and JCDecaux (in the UK from 1984), offered free shelters to local authorities in return for the right to display advertising on them, and now supply most UK shelters.

One of the pair of bus stops in Stannington (Northumberland) designed by glass engraver and architectural historian Laurence Whistler (1912–2000). They were presented to the village in 1937 by Lord Ridley of Blagdon Hall, just to the south, to commemorate the coronation of George VI. Whistler was a personal friend of the Ridleys. (Lynn Pearson)

A 1952 promotional drawing by Kirkintilloch's Lion Foundry showing the firm's regular Number 2 Bus Queue Shelter topped by a cast-iron sign directing drivers left off the busy A73 to Laidlaw's Ford dealership in Airdrie (north Lanarkshire). It was a precursor of modern bus shelter advertising. A plain Number 2 shelter survives, still in use, overlooking Holy Loch near Kilmun (Argyll and Bute). (©East Dunbartonshire Council)

4

ACCESS TO THE UNDERWORLD

Some of the most curious elements of street furniture are those we often walk on without noticing, like cast-iron coal hole covers, known technically as coal plates. Set into pavements in front of Georgian and later terrace houses with basements, they provided direct access to the coal cellars beneath for deliveries. The plate was fitted within an iron frame cemented into a hole in the paving stone. North London has some good clusters of coal plates, but they appear throughout the country; most were installed from the 1860s to the 1920s, although they are difficult to date accurately.

Coal plates are typically round, measure around a foot (0.3 m) across and bear designs, usually symmetrical and often with combinations of circles; the supplier's or ironfounder's name frequently features. These raised surfaces were intended to make the plates less

Variations on the 'four circles' coal plate design were very common. This London plate was made by Hayward Brothers, who sold it under their own name and also badged it for other suppliers. In 1865 Hayward Brothers produced six types of coal plate but ten years later this had increased to sixteen designs. (Courtesy of Philafrenzy under CC 4.0)

Above left: Coal plates supplied by builders' merchant and ironmonger Alfred Syer are found throughout Islington (London), where Syer's traded from the 1850s. The firm's warehouse was on Pentonville Road, near the Angel junction. Syer's also had a foundry to the north at the Parkhurst Works, Holloway Road, in the 1890s if not before. The firm perhaps began by using badged plates, later making its own. (Courtesy of Philafrenzy under CC 4.0)

Above right: Several coal plates in Mountjoy Square (*c*. 1790–1810), Dublin, are elaborate but anonymous. They are probably contemporary with the square, as the number of Dublin ironfounders rose from a handful in 1780 to forty-two by 1860. The city's later coal plates often came from local foundry Tonge & Taggart (established 1869); the firm usually cast its name into the plates. (Courtesy of Gavinmc in public domain)

slippery when wet. Some makers included glass elements (to illuminate the cellar) or ventilation holes as part of the design, and more complex plates incorporated a self-locking device, thus avoiding accidents to passers-by caused by missing or misaligned plates.

One of London's most important coal plate makers was Hayward Brothers of Southwark, founded in 1783 (known as Hayward Brothers & Eckstein in 1880–1916, and Haywards Ltd thereafter), which made numerous different designs. The Hayward Brothers title was included on many plates – Eckstein never seems to be mentioned – but on others it was replaced by the name of ironmongers or builders' merchants, who ordered the plates in bulk for supply to construction firms and householders. These plates were said to be badged. In addition, ironmongers sometimes made plates at their own small foundries or obtained them from ironworks in the Midlands and Scotland. Despite the loss of coal plates over the years, this has resulted in a happy variety of plate designs and maker's or merchant's names still being visible in any one street.

Hayward Brothers' coal plates can be found all over the country, but there were plenty of local makers and suppliers. Square plates are fairly common in Bristol and the north of England, as are octagonal frames in Liverpool. In areas without basements, coal might be delivered to a shed built against the inside of the backyard wall. It was accessed from the outside via a small wooden door, placed in the wall around waist height, through which the coal was tipped. Nowadays few of these evocative coal shed doors remain, but squares or rectangles of later brickwork infill are a telltale sign of their previous presence.

MANHOLE COVERS

As gas, water, sewerage and drainage networks expanded during the nineteenth century, pedestrians and traffic were increasingly inconvenienced by private companies and local authorities digging up streets. This caused – and still causes – problems countrywide. One solution, available when new roads were under construction, was to add a service subway beneath the carriageway. This took gas and water mains, drainage pipes and telegraph wires, allowing repairs to be made without the need for excavations. An early example was London's new Southwark Street (1864), where the subway was 12 ft (3.7 m) wide and 7 ft (2.1 m) high. Indeed, central London still has an extensive system of service subways, their presence occasionally given away by ventilation grids at street level.

Elsewhere, however, accessing utilities normally entailed digging trenches and using manholes. Although the traditional term manhole cover is not entirely satisfactory, it is more widely understood than any alternative. Every manhole cover protects a chamber, of

Right: Inside the service subway beneath the pavement of London's Holborn Viaduct (1863–69), from the *Illustrated London News* of 25 November 1871. It was taller but narrower than the earlier Southwark Street subway, holding water and gas mains (left) and a pipe carrying telegraph wires (right); there were connections to gas lamps and fire hydrants in the streets above. (Author's personal collection)

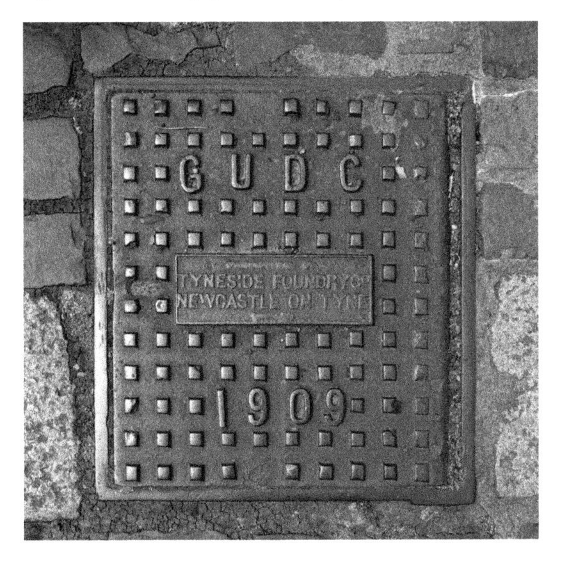

Below: This Newcastle manhole cover helpfully identifies both the former owner (Gosforth Urban District Council, established 1895) and the maker, Elswick-based Tyneside Foundry, as well as giving the date, 1909. It appears to be hinged on the right-hand side. (Lynn Pearson)

varying size and depth, which might contain drains, cables or valves, or provide physical access to sewer pipes. Beneath our pavements is a vast network of pipes and ducts, with water mains (blue pipes) generally buried below the level of gas mains (yellow pipes) and purple ducts for fibre cables. Of course, the exact position of older pipework and electrical cables is frequently unknown.

Manhole covers were usually made from cast iron, their designs often featuring the foundry name. A circular cover, for an opening measuring around 18–22 in (46–56 cm) across, weighed around 250–300 lb (113–136 kg). Square, rectangular and even triangular covers eventually became more common, some bearing names of electricity supply or tramway companies, and other utilities like Post Office Telegraphs. Modern covers come in standardised sizes and are often anonymous.

Early twentieth-century covers made by hundreds of local foundries can still be spotted throughout the UK, and the products of some larger firms, such as Needham & Sons of Stockport (Greater Manchester) and J. & S. Eyres of Manchester were installed countrywide. The number of what might be called heritage covers is constantly diminishing; foundry names are eventually worn away, and roadworks take their toll. Towards the end of the twentieth century most covers were obtained from a few major producers, notably Stanton and Staveley of Stanton by Dale (Derbyshire).

Many manhole covers in Japan are colourful works of art, initially the result of a campaign for sewer modernisation in the 1980s. The idea was taken up by local municipalities for

Above left: This well-worn specimen dates from soon after 1927, when Manchester ironfounders J. & S. Eyres were granted a patent for their non-rocking manhole cover, which prevented vibration within the frame. Although unusually heavy, it was hinged, so could be opened by a single worker. The letters 'S' and 'W' probably refer to the utility company. (Lynn Pearson)

Above right: A colourful modern Japanese manhole cover from Okayama, around 335 miles (540 km) west of Tokyo, celebrating the work of local firefighters. Around 6,000 specially designed artistic covers can now be found throughout Japan. (Courtesy of OKJaguar under CC 4.0)

Above left: A manhole cover outside Tate Liverpool, overlooking Albert Dock, installed above an existing drain as part of the 2018–19 *News from Nowhere* project and exhibition by South Korean artists Moon Kyungwon and Jeon Joonho. The artwork fulfilled British Standards manhole cover specifications. (Courtesy of Phil Nash under CC 4.0)

Above right: Workers using lifting keys in 2018 during installation of a Thames Water commemorative manhole cover. Its design celebrates the first anniversary of the destruction and removal of a giant fatberg, which blocked over 270 yds (250 m) of sewers below the site, near Whitechapel station. Note also the Transport for London manhole cover to the right. (Wrekin Products)

To mark the fiftieth anniversary of the Beatles' *Abbey Road* album in 2019, Thames Water unveiled a special manhole cover for its existing site beside the famous zebra crossing in St John's Wood, London. The commemorative cover was designed and made by Wrekin Products of Lichfield. (Wrekin Products)

publicity purposes, and the eye-catching covers now attract tourists. This approach has slowly crept into the UK, although a cover designed by the artist Antony Gormley and installed in Peckham (London) during the late 1990s was stolen. Still extant are several in central Manchester based on a classic design by local firm J. & S. Eyres, but including the words 'Right at the heart of things'. Thames Water marked the removal of the monster Whitechapel fatberg from local sewers with a commemorative manhole cover in 2018, then installed a Beatles-themed cover on London's Abbey Road the following year; both were supplied by Wrekin Products of Lichfield (Staffordshire).

PAVEMENT LIGHTS

Pavement lights are cast-iron or concrete frames holding a number of small glass blocks. Set into the pavement alongside buildings, they allow light into basement rooms beneath while providing a safe surface for pedestrian use. They often measure roughly in the region of 5 ft by 2 ft 6 in (1.5 m by 0.8 m). From the mid-nineteenth century, basement and cellar lighting for commercial premises became increasingly important as it allowed landlords to

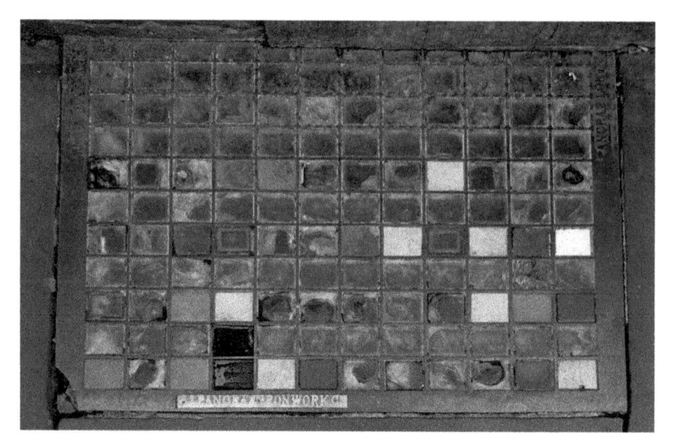

Pavement lights in Newcastle upon Tyne, made by the St Pancras Ironwork Company of King's Cross, London. The firm produced architectural ironwork from around 1860 and pavement lights by the early 1890s. Its 1897 catalogue described the company as 'basement-lighting engineers', and mentioned a recent installation in Newcastle, although this example could be a little later. (Lynn Pearson)

The product range of Hayward Brothers & Eckstein as shown inside the back cover of their *c.* 1900 catalogue, with coal plates and pavement lights to the fore. Its seventy-six pages included a colour section featuring marble and mosaic frames in combinations of red, white, orange, grey and black, but few of these survive. (Collection of Ian Macky)

A medium-sized installation of 1920s pavement lights by leading makers Haywards, in London's Portobello Road (Notting Hill). A similar arrangement of frame and 4 in by 3 in (102 mm by 76 mm) prisms appeared in the firm's *c.* 1929 catalogue, the maximum regular size being sixteen lights across by thirteen deep; larger frames could be specially ordered. (Lynn Pearson)

Tiled pavement lights, probably from the 1920s, by Thaddeus Hyatt & Co. of Farringdon Road, London. The maker is named (inverted) near the top centre of the frame. The lenses change colour over time, as exposure to ultraviolet light affects impurities in the glass, turning it purple or pale yellow. (Lynn Pearson)

charge higher rents, while occupiers spent less on artificial lighting. However, plain slabs of glass proved to be inefficient light transmitters, and it was the introduction of glass prisms by Hayward Brothers of Southwark, the coal plate manufacturers, in 1871 that transformed the pavement lighting business.

Hayward's patent prism lights bent the incoming light through ninety degrees, directing it effectively into basement areas. Their popularity spawned a raft of competitors, including the American Thaddeus Hyatt, whose Lens Light Works stood in London's Farringdon Road from the 1870s until the Second World War. By the 1890s Hyatt's lights were in use at all the City of London's underground public conveniences. Lavish catalogues issued by pavement light makers featured lengthy lists of jobs successfully executed throughout the UK, for instance the hundred or so premises in London's Old and New Bond Streets supplied by Hayward Brothers. Otherwise, their contents were similar, with a succession of differently shaped glass elements and frames alternatively finished with mosaic, marble or cement. Frames normally included the maker's name.

By the 1930s electric lighting had reduced the impact of pavement lights, although they remain in use today; concrete-framed pavement lights are now the norm, although iron-framed lights are still manufactured. Many traditional pavement lights, mostly dating from the 1890s to the 1920s, survive in commercial areas of our towns and cities, their maker's names slowly being worn away by the passage of feet.

VENTILATION SHAFTS

Ventilation shafts are essential for the proper functioning of tunnels; they carry heat away from electric cables and other sources, as well as providing fresh air and removing fumes. Many vent shafts, particularly those of canal and railway tunnels, are located deep in the countryside, although a few canal vents can be found in the streets of the West Midlands. In addition, shafts in cities, notably London, are often disguised as or hidden by structures that are best described as architecture rather than street furniture, and fall outside the scope of this book. However, there are still many smaller vent shafts, both historic and modern, to be seen on our streets.

In section two (see page 44) we considered turn-of-the-century sewer vent pipes, most of which are lamp-post-like cast-iron columns, occasionally with decorative heads. A few vents for tunnels of railway or electricity undertakings remain from the same era and look quite similar to sewer vents. In Aberdeen, for instance, two rail tunnel vent shafts made by Macfarlane's Saracen Foundry survive north of the centre in Hutcheon Street. Dating from around 1900, they resemble lamp posts with very elaborate crowns, and were probably sold by the foundry as multipurpose columns. Curiously, they are quite unlike the contemporary art nouveau vent shaft around half a mile (0.8 km) to the south, also by Macfarlane's and serving an electricity network tunnel.

This startling art nouveau ventilator shaft (*c.* 1905) at the west end of Justice Mill Lane, Aberdeen, was made by Macfarlane's Saracen Foundry; the concrete base is modern. The cast-iron column served an extant cable subway running around 1,500 yds (1,370 m) to the former Corporation electricity works and tram car depot, south of the city's railway station. (Rachel Martin)

The Oxford foundry Lucy's manufactured stubby, circular vent shafts with vertical grilles at the head, some of which were used in Leeds during the mid-twentieth century. Several shafts from the same period, in the form of small louvred cabinets, survive in Glasgow where they cooled a network of cable-carrying tunnels related to a major telephone exchange. In London, at the junction of Leather Lane and Holborn, is an odd hexagonal vent shaft with seating at its base. It stands over 20 ft (6 m) in height with vent grilles top and bottom, and serves the huge former Kingsway telephone exchange below, sited in a group of 1940s and 1950s tunnels.

Modern vent shafts, linked to tunnels and underground car parks, can take many forms, but vents-cum-public artworks by well-known artists are often seen in major developments. They can be found outside the capital, but London boasts a good collection, including Jeff Bell's *Cast Glass Panels* (1992), cladding car park vents at the four corners of Cabot Square, Canary Wharf. In the City of London, the Heatherwick Studio's 36-ft-high (11 m) stainless steel *Paternoster Vents* (2002) provide cooling for an electricity substation below Paternoster Square, north of St Paul's Cathedral.

Above left: The so-called Camberwell Submarine on Akerman Road in south London provides ventilation for the sub-surface boiler plant of a district heating system serving the Myatts Fields estates (*c.* 1970–78, partly redeveloped). Eminent structural engineer Edmund 'Ted' Happold (1930–96) advised Lambeth's Architect's Department on the boiler house design. (Courtesy of Jwslubbock under CC 4.0)

Above right: The roughly 10-ft-high (3 m) *Parsons' Polygon* (1982–85, artist David Hamilton) in the centre of Newcastle upon Tyne is actually a vent for the Metro rail tunnel beneath. The concrete ventilation shaft is clad in terracotta panels bearing designs derived from the working drawings of locally based engineer Sir Charles Parsons (1854–1931), developer of steam turbine engines. (Lynn Pearson)

Above left: Close to London's Pimlico Tube station stands the robot-like sculpture *Pimlico Cooling Tower* (1978–82) by Eduardo Paolozzi (1924–2005). Aluminium-painted, cast-iron panels form cladding around the base of what is actually a ventilation shaft for a nearby commercial development's underground car park. (Lynn Pearson)

Above right: Two of the three huge ventilation shafts – 'earth tubes' – at the Co-op Group's headquarters One Angel Square (2010–13, architects 3DReid), Manchester. The shafts act as chimneys for its natural ventilation system, allowing fresh air into the sixteen-storey building, which boasts a high degree of environmental sustainability. (Lynn Pearson)

A panoramic night-time view of Cabot Square in London's Canary Wharf, with the four illuminated cylinders of Jeff Bell's *Cast Glass Panels* (1992) occupying the corners. They enhance the streetscape while providing ventilation for the car park beneath the square. (IndustryAndTravel/Bigstock.com)

5

FUTURE STREETS

Before the Covid-19 pandemic, ideas about the future development of our streets focused on improvements to environmental quality, with enhanced digital connectivity as a useful additional benefit. The pandemic brought other matters to the fore. Initially, a profusion of 'Thank You NHS' rainbows appeared on roads, walls, windows and even trees. The need for people to keep their distance from one another then resulted in short-term, rapid alterations to street layouts. Increased space was allocated to cyclists and pedestrians by means of construction barriers, planters and bollards. Abundant traffic cones – essentially portable bollards – changed the appearance of the streets, although perhaps only on a temporary basis.

The traffic cone is a relatively new invention, arriving from America in the late 1950s and first used on the M6 – originally they were wood or concrete. Today's ubiquitous rubber or plastic cones come in sizes typically ranging from 1 ft 8 in to 3 ft 4 in (0.5 to 1.0 m) in height and weighing 5–15 lb (2.5–7 kg). One estimate suggests that there are

In June 2020, during the pandemic, Network Rail commissioned 'Thank You NHS' designs for over seventy bollards outside the south entrance to London Bridge station on St Thomas Street (Southwark). The bollards had previously featured other artworks, including local photographs in 2017. (Courtesy of Ethan Doyle White under CC 4.0)

well over 1.3 million cones in the UK, some of them green, yellow or blue as well as the familiar orange. The number is still increasing, as the cones have now been joined by rather slimmer polyurethane columns known as delineators, which serve to mark out cycle lanes while taking up less road space.

GREENING THE STREETS

Urban tree planting and living walls are accepted methods of removing carbon from the atmosphere and reducing air pollution. Environmentally friendly street furniture is now being made with the same aims. In London's Belgravia, lamp posts were fitted with vegetation panels in 2019 to improve air quality; although this was a trial, if successful the panels could be fixed to many of the city's 350,000 lamp posts. On a larger scale, two German-designed pollution-reducing 'moss trees', the UK's first, were installed in Glasgow during 2017. The moss tree is a 13 ft (4 m) high, moss-filled slab-like wall with seating at its base; one moss tree is said to be as efficient as around 275 trees in terms of pollution reduction. In 2018, moss trees were tested in Newcastle and central London, and two more sited permanently at Leytonstone (London) in late 2019.

A simpler green intervention is the micro-park or parklet, which provides seating – often sculptural, brightly coloured or both – alongside zones of planting to create pockets of public space. Some parklets can now be seen along London's Tooley Street. In more complex schemes, entire streets can be transformed with the introduction of wider pavements, high-quality surfaces, new lighting and substantial planters, as in London's

The tall green panel beyond the equestrian monument (1844) to the Duke of Wellington is one of Glasgow's two moss trees, installed in Royal Exchange Square during 2017 to help reduce pollution. A traffic cone has adorned the statue's head since the 1980s and is now something of a tourist attraction. (Jeff Whyte Photography/Bigstock.com)

England's first moss tree was installed by Northumbrian Water at Newcastle upon Tyne's Haymarket during reconstruction of a complex road junction in 2018. It was removed after seventeen months of filtering pollutants, having collected much useful data on air quality. (Northumbrian Water)

Colourful patterned seating and planters by French designer Camille Walala were introduced to London's South Molton Street (Mayfair) during 2019. The pedestrianised street, which previously had no public seating, became the Walala Lounge, an 'urban living room'. (Lynn Pearson)

A London taxi using an electric vehicle charging point in Russell Square (Camden), handily sited near one of the historic cabmen's shelters, out of view to the left. At the start of 2021 there were at least thirteen major charging networks in the UK, the largest being ubitricity with its lamp post chargers. (Courtesy of Philafrenzy under CC 4.0)

South Molton Street. A similar project is planned for Newcastle's historic Grey Street, giving cyclists and pedestrians extra space. Greener streets also mean more charging points for e-bikes and electric vehicles. The current generation of electric vehicle roadside charging points for public use tend to be white or green cabinets around 6 ft (1.8 m) in height, with space for multiple connections, although some are incorporated into existing street lights.

DIGITAL CONNECTIVITY

We are beginning to see more digital street furniture. The old town plan on its upright panel is being overtaken by the digital 'totem', a tall stand with an interactive map that also offers Wi-Fi and device charging. Litter bins may now be smart bins, with sensors that alert management when they need emptying. Massive digital advertising screens, some several storeys in height, are appearing in city centres. The humble bus stop can even become a digital hub. In 2016 a new bus shelter was piloted at the Paton Street stop on Manchester's Piccadilly; it included interactive information screens, Wi-Fi, device charging and a broad, green-planted roof. There will doubtless be much more digital street furniture. Even something as simple as a bench can incorporate ample opportunities for advertising and data collection.

Phone apps, providing maps and information, assist with the charity art trails that began to appear in the UK following Chicago's 1999 CowParade. Hosts of animal sculptures, all decorated by different artists, invade the streets to encourage donations before being auctioned for charity. This new take on old collecting boxes was seen in locations including Norwich (2013, elephants), Birmingham (2015, owls), Suffolk (2016, pigs), the Lake District (2016, sheep) and Manchester (2018, bees). A hybrid of temporary street furniture and public art, such events bring colour and public involvement to our streets.

6

WHAT NEXT?

FURTHER READING

Brief introductions to street furniture include the attractive, pocket-sized *Hard Furnishings* (2002) by Peter Ashley and *Street Furniture* (1987) by Henry Aaron. The capital is surveyed in *London Street Furniture* (2010) by David Brandon and Alan Brooke. For a splendid exploration of iron street furniture, see Paul Dobraszczyk's *Iron, Ornament and Architecture in Victorian Britain* (2014). Modern street furniture is analysed from an academic perspective in Eleanor Herring's *Street Furniture Design: Contesting Modernism in Post-War Britain* (2017). An interesting worldwide guide to street furniture and design is *The 99% Invisible City* (2020) by Roman Mars and Kurt Kohlstedt.

A good overview of recent research on Roman roads and milestones is given by M. C. Bishop's *The Secret History of the Roman Roads of Britain* (2014), while *Roman Roads in Britain* (2008) by Hugh Davies provides a well-illustrated and enjoyable summary. Mervyn Benford's *Milestones* (2002) is a compact and visually attractive survey of the subject. The history of road signage is dealt with in great detail by John Willrich's excellent *Did You Notice the Signs by the Way?* (2013), while *Road Signs* (2002) by Stuart Hands is a useful and attractive brief history. In addition, the magisterial *Carscapes* (2012) by Kathryn A. Morrison and John Minnis includes several helpful sections on road signage and related matters. Alistair Hall's beautifully produced *London Street Signs* (2020) is a visual history of the city's street nameplates, while Anton Tantner's *House Numbers* (2015) is an informative and nicely illustrated guide.

Village Pumps (2009) by Richard K. Williams gives a detailed overview of the world of pumps, while *Troughs and Drinking Fountains* (1989) by Philip Davies is a well-produced introduction to the topic. A major work on public conveniences is the beautiful *Temples of Convenience and Chambers of Delight* (2007) by Lucinda Lambton.

Jonathan Glancey's *Pillar Boxes* (1989) is an authoritative short text with very useful illustrations. In *The Irish Post Box* (2009), Stephen Ferguson gives us an illustrated account of the postbox in the Republic of Ireland. A thorough guide to the design history of the telephone box, including those used by various emergency services, is *The British Phonebox* (2017) by Nigel Linge and Andy Sutton, while Gavin Stamp's *Telephone Boxes* (1989) is an excellent illustrated guide to the subject.

Manhole and coal hole covers of London (mostly) and Sheffield respectively are shown and described in Gillian Cooksey's excellent *Artistry and History Underfoot* (2008) and

Drainspotting: A Guide to the Pavement Features of Sheffield (2014) by Calvin Payne and Andy Cooper. For London see *Inventive Vents* (2021) by Lucy Lavers.

New London Architecture's publication *Future Streets* (2019), available to download from https://nla.london/insights/future-streets, is an attractive consideration of potential new infrastructure.

Useful illustrated guides to elements of street furniture beyond the scope of this book are: *Fountains and Water Features* (2009) by Rosalind Hopwood, *War Memorials* (2019) by Roger Bowdler, *London's Statues and Monuments* (2018) by Peter Matthews and *Public Art since 1950* (2006) by Lynn Pearson.

Finally, *England in Particular* (2006) by Sue Clifford and Angela King is an alphabetically arranged cornucopia of the local, the everyday, the unusual and the distinctive, with many entries of interest to students of street furniture.

USEFUL WEBSITES

Historic England (historicengland.org.uk) has several relevant publications, particularly the street furniture listing selection guide: historicengland.org.uk/images-books/publications/dlsg-street-furniture/.

Scotland's Building Conservation Centre, the Engine Shed (engineshed.scot/publications) is the gateway to many useful publications available online, including catalogues of several historic ironfounders.

The website roads.org.uk provides a vast amount of information about Britain's road network, including a great deal on road signs and typefaces. Similarly, the website simoncornwell.com/lighting/home.htm is hugely informative on the history of street lighting. Locations of Ordnance Survey benchmarks are available at ordnancesurvey.co.uk/benchmarks.

Much detail on water pumps, and many illustrations, can be found on the comprehensive website villagepumps.org.uk/index.html. The searchable blog memorialdrinkingfountains.wordpress.com contains images and details of around 400 fountains worldwide, including many in the UK.

A plethora of information on telephone boxes, AA and RAC boxes, and other street furniture can be found at the well-illustrated enthusiast website the-telephone-box.co.uk.

Many catalogues of historic pavement light manufacturers can be found at glassian.org/library.html.

GET INVOLVED

The Milestone Society is a charity concerned with recording, research, conservation and restoration of milestones and other waymarkers. Its helpful website (milestonesociety.co.uk) has numerous links to maps of milestone locations and photographs. Members have helped to restore hundreds of milestones and continue to catalogue their details; currently over 31,000 examples have been located.

The Letter Box Study Group is an independent authority on letter boxes with an active membership. It maintains a database of letter box locations and attributes. Its website (lbsg.org) includes many photographs and detailed descriptions of box types. Members carry out surveys of boxes, research undocumented examples and contribute to recording.